GRAPHIC ORNAMENTS

GRAPHISCHE ORNAMENTE • ORNAMENTOS GRAFICOS • ORNEMENTS GRAPHIQUES • ORNAMENTI GRAFICI

1900

GRAPHIC ORNAMENTS

GRAPHISCHE ORNAMENTE · ORNAMENTOS GRAFICOS · ORNEMENTS GRAPHIQUES · ORNAMENTI GRAFICI

1900

THE PEPIN PRESS

Copyright for this edition © 1995, 1996 The Pepin Press B/v
First published in 1995 by The Pepin Press
Copyright introduction 'Graphic Ornaments 1900' © 1995, 1996 Pepin Van Roojen
Translations: Anette Diekmann, Susanne Friedrich, Adolfo Estevez and
Taalcentrum-VU

ISBN 90 5496 011 6

The Pepin Press
POB 10349
1001 EH Amsterdam
Fax (+) 31 20 4201152

GRAPHIC ORNAMENTS 1900

The greater part of the 19th century in Europe was not a particularly fertile period with regard to original ornamental design — rather, it was a time during which styles of the past were used again. Examples of this are the Gothic Revival, which started in the late 18th century and continued well into the 19th century, and a number of neo-styles.

In the wake of colonialism and trade between Europe and the Middle and Far East, decorative arts from the Orient became popular in the second half of the 19th century. Especially Japanese ornamental influence became distinct, receiving a strong impetus from the London International Exhibition of 1862, where many Japanese items were on display. An increasing number of publications on Japanese design appeared around the same time. Typical of Japanese ornamental style are serene compositions of elements of nature (water, clouds, lotuses, flowers, etcetera), often in pastel colour schemes.

Only by the end of the 19th century did a truly new European style emerge: Art Nouveau, or *Jugendstil.* This style certainly owes to the neo-styles popular at that time, but more so to Oriental, in particular Japanese, design. Typical Japanese elements, such as the use of wave and cloud-like forms and floral and plant motifs, have inspired European artists to experiment with organic shapes and general curvilinear design, giving the decorative arts during the Art Nouveau period

an until then uncommon spontaneous appeal.

Also, in the late 19th century — the time of the Industrial Revolution — typefoundries and printing equipment rapidly became more advanced, making it possible to reproduce more complicated or intricate designs in print. And, in addition, printed materials could easily be produced in larger quantities. Similar developments took place in, for instance, the textile and furniture industry, causing the Art Nouveau decorative style to spread very quickly throughout Europe, penetrating practically every aspect of material culture.

However, the revival styles of the 19th century did not disappear immediately; at around 1900 they were still being used for the decoration of a wide variety of items, alongside Art Nouveau and imitations of Oriental design. One of the results of these various styles being used at the same time was the experiment with eclectic styles. So it is possible to recognize in certain graphic embellishments Gothic or Renaissance elements in combination with Oriental ones.

The thousands of ornaments presented here were all created in the latter part of the 19th century and the first two decades of the 20th century, and provide a comprehensive overview of the motifs used at that time for the decoration of printed materials.

GRAPHISCHE ORNAMENTE UM 1900

Im Laufe des 19. Jahrhunderts sind in Europa nur wenige neue Ornamente geschaffen worden. In dieser Zeit wurden eher Ornamente und Stilrichtungen vergangener Epochen wiederentdeckt. Ein Beispiel hierfür ist das Wiederaufleben gothischer Elemente am Ende des 18. Jahrhundert bis ins 19. Jahrhundert oder eine Reihe anderer sogenannter Neo-Stilrichtungen.

Infolge der Kolonialisierung und des zunehmenden Handels zwischen Europa und dem Nahen und Fernen Osten erlangt in der zweiten Hälfte des 19. Jahrhunderts besonders die dekorative Kunst der asiatischen Länder außerordentliche Popularität. Nach dem großen Erfolg auf der Weltausstellung in London im Jahre 1862, wo viele japanische Objekte ausgestellt wurden, wird der Einfluß japanischer Ornamente besonders deutlich. Zur gleichen Zeit nimmt die Zahl der Publikationen über Japanisches Design zu. Typisch für den Stil japanischer Ornamente sind ruhige, klare und heitere Kompositionen natürlicher Elemente (Wasser, Wolken, Lotusblüten, Blumen, etc), die meistens in Pasteltönen gehalten werden.

Erst gegen Ende des 19. Jahrhunderts kommt es in Europa zu einer wirklich neuen Stilrichtung: der Jugendstil oder *Art Nouveau*. Dieser geht auf die derzeit beliebten Neo-Stilrichtungen und in weitaus größerem Maße auf asiatische und insbesondere japanische Formen zurück. Typische japanische Elemente wie z.B. Wellen- oder Wolkenformen oder Blumen- und Pflanzenmotive haben die europäischen Künstler inspiriert, mit organischen und allgemein weichen und

kurvenreichen Formen zu experimentieren und verleihen den dekorativen Kunstformen des Jugendstils eine bis dahin ungewöhnliche Eigenwirkung.

Während der Industriellen Revolution am Ende des 19. Jahrhunderts werden Setzer- und Druckereinrichtungen erheblich modernisiert, was den Druck und darüberhinaus auch die Vervielfältigung weitaus komplizierterer Muster ermöglicht. Parallele Entwicklungen zeigen sich auch in der Textil- und Möbelindustrie. So konnte sich der Jugendstil schnell in ganz Europa verbreiten und nahezu alle Formen der dekorativen Kunst durchdringen.

Dennoch geraten die im 19. Jahrhundert wiederentdeckten Elemente früherer Stilrichtungen nicht unmittelbar wieder in den Hintergrund, sondern werden um 1900 weiterhin zusammen mit dem Jugendstil und neben den vielfachen Imitationen asiatischer Formen zur Verzierung vieler Gegenstände verwendet. Die unterschiedlichen Stilrichtungen werden miteinander kombiniert. Daher sind zum Beispiel in bestimmten graphischen Verzierungen Elemente der Gothik oder der Renaissance mit asiatischen Elementen verbunden.

In diesem Buch werden mehr als dreitausend Ornamente wiedergegeben, die alle gegen Ende des 19. Jahrhunderts und in den ersten zwei Jahrzehnten des 20. Jahrhunderts geschaffen wurden. Sie geben einen umfassenden Überblick über die Motive, die in dieser Zeit für Gestaltung und Verzierung von *Gedrucktem* verwendet wurden.

ORNAMENTOS GRAFICOS EN 1900

A lo largo del siglo XIX se crearon en Europa pocos ornamentos nuevos; más bien fueron redescubiertos ornamentos y estilos de épocas pasadas, como lo muestra el renacimiento de elementos góticas a finales del siglo XVIII y principios del siglo XIX o una serie de los así llamados neoestilos.

Como consecuencia de la colonización y del aumento del comercio entre Europa y el Oriente, en la segunda mitad del siglo XIX, el arte decorativo de los países asiáticos adquiere particularmente popularidad. Tras el gran éxito en la Exposición Universal de Londres en 1862, donde muchos objetos japoneses fueron expuestos, la influencia de los ornamentos japoneses se hace especialmente presente. Simultáneamente aumentan las publicaciones sobre diseño japonés. Características típicas del estilo de los ornamentos japoneses son las composiciones serenas, diáfanas y alegres de elementos de la naturaleza (agua, nubes, flores de lotos y otras flores etc.), utilizándose principalmente tonos pastel.

Tan sólo a finales del siglo XIX aparece en Europa un estilo verdaderamente nuevo, el Art Nouveau, o *Jugendstil*. Este estilo tiene seguramente sus raíces en los neoestilos populares en la época, pero en mayor medida está influído por formas asiáticas, particularmente japonesas. Elementos típicos japoneses como olas o nubes así como motivos de flores o plantas inspiraron a los artistas europeos a

LE DESSIN
D'ORNEMENTATION
VERS 1900

experimentar con formas orgánicas y en general con diseños suaves y ondulados, otorgándole al arte decorativo durante el período del Art Nouveau un efecto propio, inédito hasta el momento.

Durante la Revolución Industrial a finales del siglo XIX los talleres de tipografía e imprentas son modernizados considerablemente, permitiendo la impresión y además la multiplicación de diseños de mayor complejidad. En la industria textil y de muebles se produce un desarollo similar. De ahí que el Art Nouveau logará expandirse con gran rapidez por toda Europa imponiéndose practicamente en todas las formas del arte decorativo.

A pesar de ello, los elementos del pasado redescubiertos en el siglo XIX no desaparecen inmediatamente, se siguen usando alrededor de 1900 junto con el Art Nouveau y las numerosas imitaciones de formas asiáticas, en la decoración de muchos objetos. Se combinan los diferentes estilos entre sí de modo que se encuentran por ejemplo en determinados adornos gráficos elementos góticos o renacentistas combinados con elementos asiáticos.

En este libro se reproducen más de tres mil ornamentos, todos los cuales fueron creados a finales del siglo XIX y en los primeros decenios del siglo XX. Muestran una visión extensa de los motivos usados en esta época para el diseño y la decoración de materiales impresos.

En matière de dessin d'ornementation, le XIXème siècle n'a pas, dans son ensemble, été une période particulièrement fertile; elle se caractérise plutôt par la remise au goût du jour de styles anciens. Parmi ceux-ci, le style «néo-gothique», qui voit le jour à la fin du XVIIIème siècle et se répand jusqu'au-delà de 1850, accompagné d'un foisonnement d'autres styles affublés du préfixe «néo».

C'est grâce à la colonalisation et au commerce avec l'Extrême Orient que les arts décoratifs orientaux connaissent un grand succès en Europe dans la deuxième moitié du XIXème. De tous ceux-ci, c'est sans nul doute l'influence japonaise, promue par l'Exposition Internationale de Londres de 1862, où furent présentés une multitude d'objets de ce pays, qui se fera le plus sentir. Témoin le nombre croissant de publications sur le design japonais qui commencent à circuler à peu près au même moment. Dans les grandes lignes, on dira du style ornemental japonais qu'il se distingue par ses compositions, d'une grande sérénité, d'éléments de la nature (eau, nuages, lotus, fleurs, etc.), souvent en couleurs pastel.

Il faut attendre la fin du XIXème siècle pour voir l'émergence d'un style réellement européen : l'Art Nouveau, ou *Jugendstil*. Bien qu'influencé par les styles «néo» qui fleurissent à l'époque, ce mouvement doit avant tout sa filiation aux styles orientaux, particulièrement au design japonais. C'est en effet à partir d'éléments typiquement japonais, tels que des formes évoquant des vagues ou des nuages ou encore des motifs floraux et végétaux, que les artistes européens se

sont mis à expérimenter sur des figures organiques et sur un dessin généralement curvilinéaire, insufflant dans les arts décoratifs de l'Art Nouveau un caractère spontané inconnu jusqu'alors.

Et c'est également au crépuscule du XIXème siècle — à l'ère de la Révolution industrielle — que les progrès réalisés dans les techniques de fonderie et d'impression permettent de reproduire et d'imprimer des motifs plus compliqués. Parallèlement, il devient possible de produire les imprimés en plus grandes quantités. Des progrès tout à fait comparables sont aussi enregistrés dans l'industrie textile et de l'ameublement, permettant au style décoratif de l'Art Nouveau de se répandre très rapidement en Europe, et de s'introduire dans pratiquement chaque aspect de la culture «matérielle».

Toutefois, les styles «néo» qui jalonnent le XIXème siècle n'ont pas pour autant disparu: vers 1900, ils ont toujours cours, en décoration, aux côté de l'Art Nouveau et d'imitations de design oriental. La combinaison d'éléments issus de ces mouvements a donné naissance à ce que l'on a appelé le style éclectique. C'est ainsi qu'il est possible de distinguer, dans certains ornements, des éléments gothiques ou Renaissance, conjugués à des éléments orientaux.

Les milliers d'ornements présentés ici ont tous été créés à la fin du XIXème siècle et durant les deux premières decennies du XXème; ils fournissent un aperçu assez exhaustif des motifs utilisés à cette époque dans la décoration de matières imprimées.

GRAFICA ORNAMENTALE DEL 1900

Nel campo della grafica ornamentale originale, il XIX secolo non rappresenta un periodo particolarmente fertile; quasi tutto il secolo è, al contrario, caratterizzato da un ritorno agli stili del passato. Chiari esempi sono la Rinascita Gotica, iniziata nel tardo XVIII secolo e durata fino all'800 inoltrato, e diversi 'neo-stili'.

Sulla scia del colonialismo e del fiorente commercio tra l'Europa e il Medio e l'Estremo Oriente, nella seconda metà del XIX secolo le arti decorative orientali acquistarono popolarità. Soprattutto l'influenza dell'ornamentalismo giapponese divenne chiaramente avvertibile, in seguito anche al forte impulso dato dall'Esposizione Internazionale di Londra del 1862, nella quale vennero esposti molti pezzi giapponesi. All'incirca nello stesso periodo vide la luce un crescente numero di pubblicazioni sul design grafico giapponese. Tipiche dell'arte decorativa giapponese sono le serene composizioni con elementi tratti dalla natura (acqua, nuvole, loto, fiori ecc.), spesso realizzati in schemi cromatici con tenui tinte pastello.

Solo verso la fine del XIX secolo cominciò a delinearsi un autentico nuovo stile europeo, l'Art Nouveau o *Jugendstil*; è uno stile indubbiamente orientato verso le neo-tendenze allora in auge, ma forse in misura ancora maggiore verso la grafica decorativa orientale, in particolare quella giapponese. I tipici elementi dell'arte giapponese — come le forme ispirate alle onde e alle nubi, o i motivi floreali e di piante — hanno ispirato gli artisti europei a cimentarsi con forme organiche e con il tipico stile prevalentemente curvilineo che conferisce a tutte le opere decorative realizzate nel periodo dell'Art Nouveau un'inconfondibile e spontanea carica estetica.

Nel tardo Ottocento — nel periodo cioè della Rivoluzione Industriale — anche le fonderie di caratteri e le macchine da stampa progredirono rapidamente, diventando sempre più avanzate e rendendo così possibile riprodurre motivi e disegni più complessi o più intricati. Inoltre, il materiale stampato poteva facilmente essere prodotto in tirature più elevate. Un'evoluzione analoga si verificò, ad esempio, nel settore tessile e dei mobili. Questi sviluppi portarono ad una rapida diffusione in tutt'Europa dello stile decorativo dell'Art Nouveau, che penetrò praticamente in ogni manifestazione della cultura dei materiali.

Gli stili 'risorti' in uso nel XIX secolo non scomparvero comunque subito: intorno al 1900 venivano infatti ancora usati per la decorazione di una grande varietà di oggetti, parallelamente all'Art Nouveau e alle imitazioni della grafica decorativa orientale. Uno dei prodotti dell'uso contestuale di stili diversi è il fenomeno degli stili eclettici: esperimenti di armonizzazione in seguito ai quali è oggi possibile, ad esempio, riscontrare in alcune decorazioni grafiche elementi gotici o rinascimentali abbinati a motivi orientali.

Tutti i motivi presentati in questo libro — alcune migliaia — sono stati creati negli ultimi decenni del XIX secolo e nei primi due del XX, e forniscono un quadro completo dei motivi usati in quel periodo per la decorazione di materiali stampati.

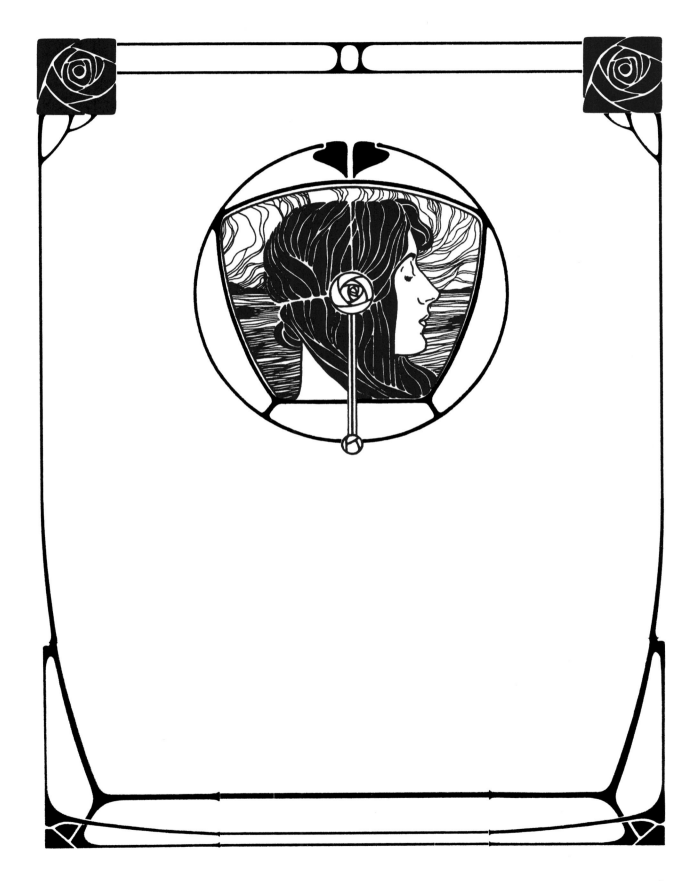

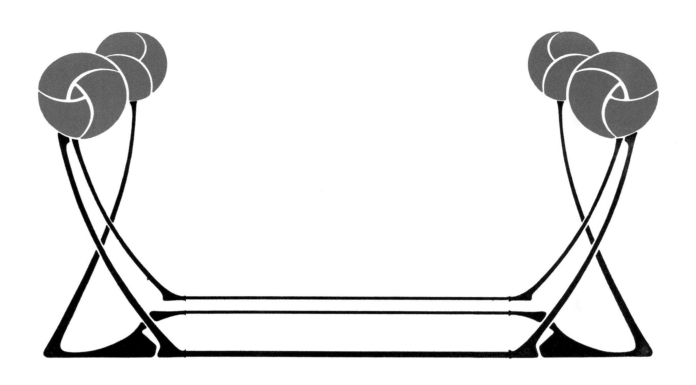

BAUGEWERBE AUSSTELLUNG
IM MUSEUM ZU MÜNCHEN

TANZKARTE

BERLINER
KÜNSTLER
BUND

SOMMERFEST
1904

HUMOR

TAFELKARTE

HARMONIA

NORDHEIM

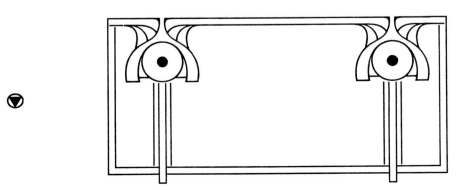

TANZ KARTE

POLONAISE MIT
WALZER
TYROLIENNE
RHEINLÄNDER

PAUSE

POLKA D.-WAHL
SCHOTTISCH
CONTRE
QUODLIBET

ABENDS ·
ACHT UHR
LAMPION

JAHRESFEST
ROSE   GRAZ

SPEISE   KARTE

SUPPE MIT EINLAGE

⊛ STEINBUTT ⊛

REHBRATEN MIT
REMOULADENSAUCE

⊛ NACHTISCH ⊛

WITH HEARTY GREETING
AND SINCERE GOOD WISHES

NEW YEAR 1905

PROBATICO

DE MADERA, HULES, ETC., PARA LUSTRARLOS BIEN
CON EL RELAMPAGO PRODUCTO, DE RESULTADO IM-
MEJORABLE, DE FACIL USO Y MUY ECONOMICO · VARIOS
COLORES · UNICO DEPOSITO

DROGUERIA DE MORENO, MAYOR, 135

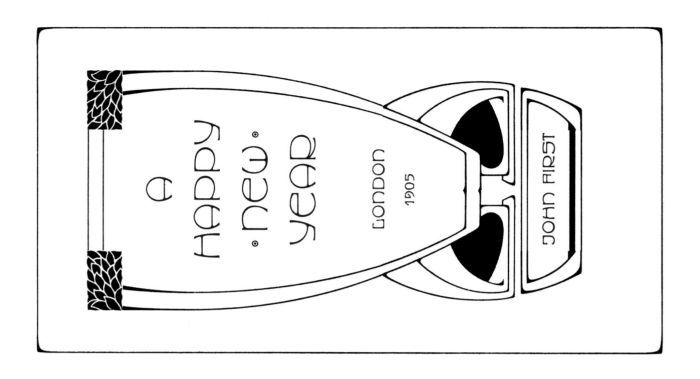

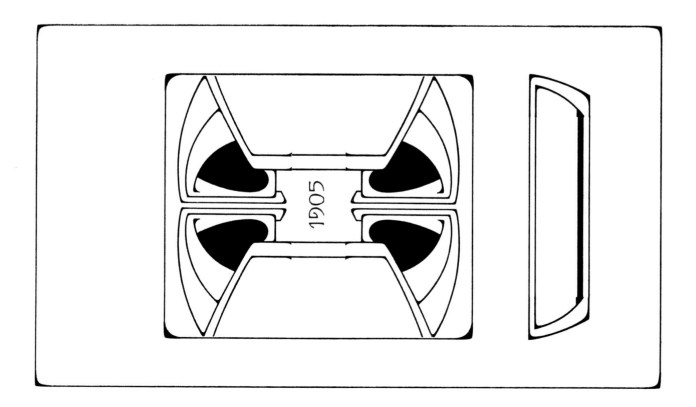

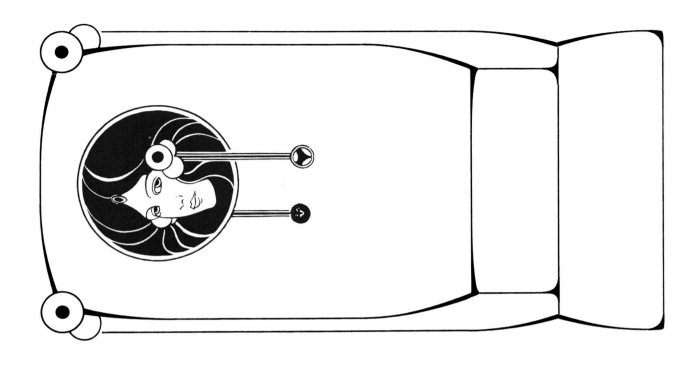

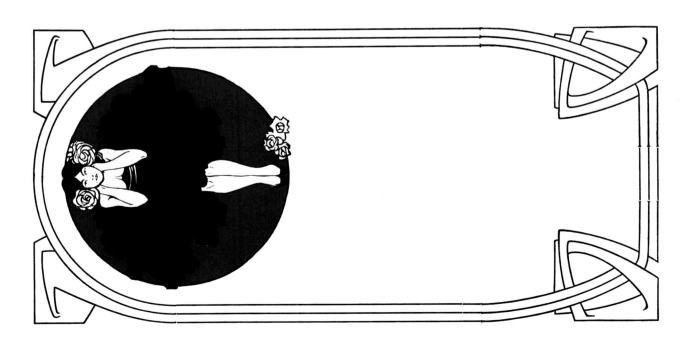

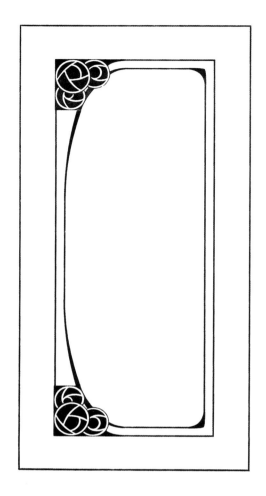

KONGO-THEE
DIREKTER IMPORT

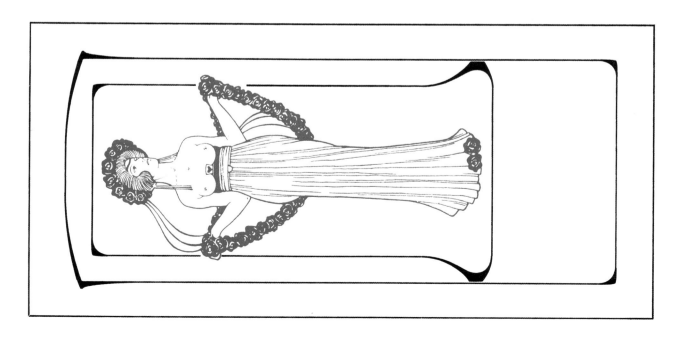

DEUTSCHE HUTFABRIK

Permanente Ausstellung
Asia-Haus

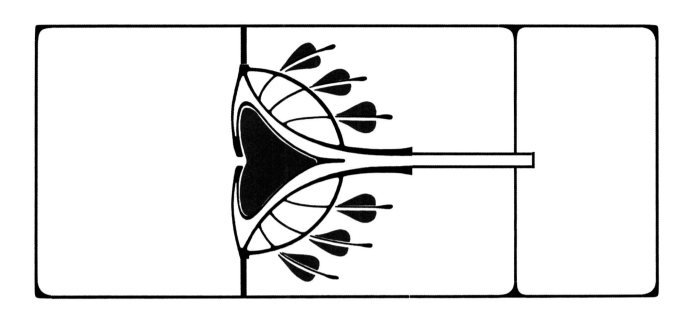

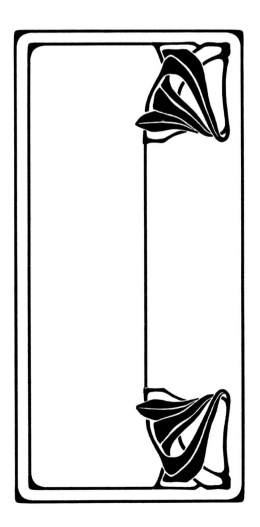

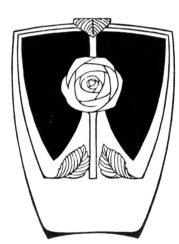

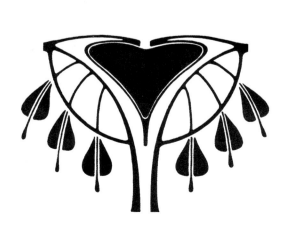

JUAN CABALLERO

MADRID · BILBAO

IMPORTADOR DE MAQUINARIA PARA LA INDUSTRIA

REPRESENTANTE

J. G. SCHELTER Y GIESECKE · LEIPZIG

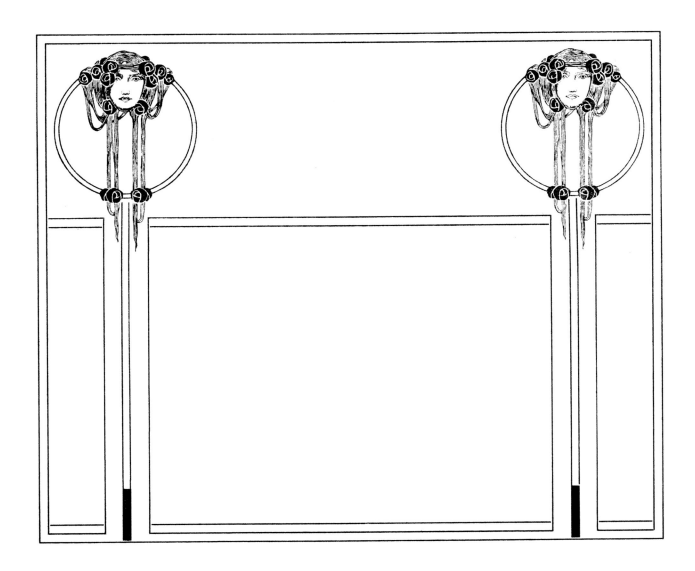

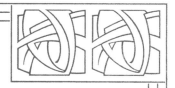

ZIERSCHRIFT
EDDA

PRAKTISCHE GESCHENKE | ENDE PROGRAMM MUSIK
PROLOG GESANG | WIDMUNG 24 BALLADEN

HOCHZEITSSCHERZ 19 POSTKARTENPOEM
HARMONIE NOTENSCHULE MANDOLINE

POESIE TANZORDNUNG ALBUM
GRAPHISCHE VEREINIGUNG

MÜNCHENER KALENDER
SOUPER TOASTE

BESUCHSANZEIGE

AUGENMIMIK

SCHRIFTGIESSEREI   PARIS 1900: GRAND PRIX   MASCHINENFABRIK

J. G. SCHELTER & GIESECKE

EDDA-ZEILENFÜLLER

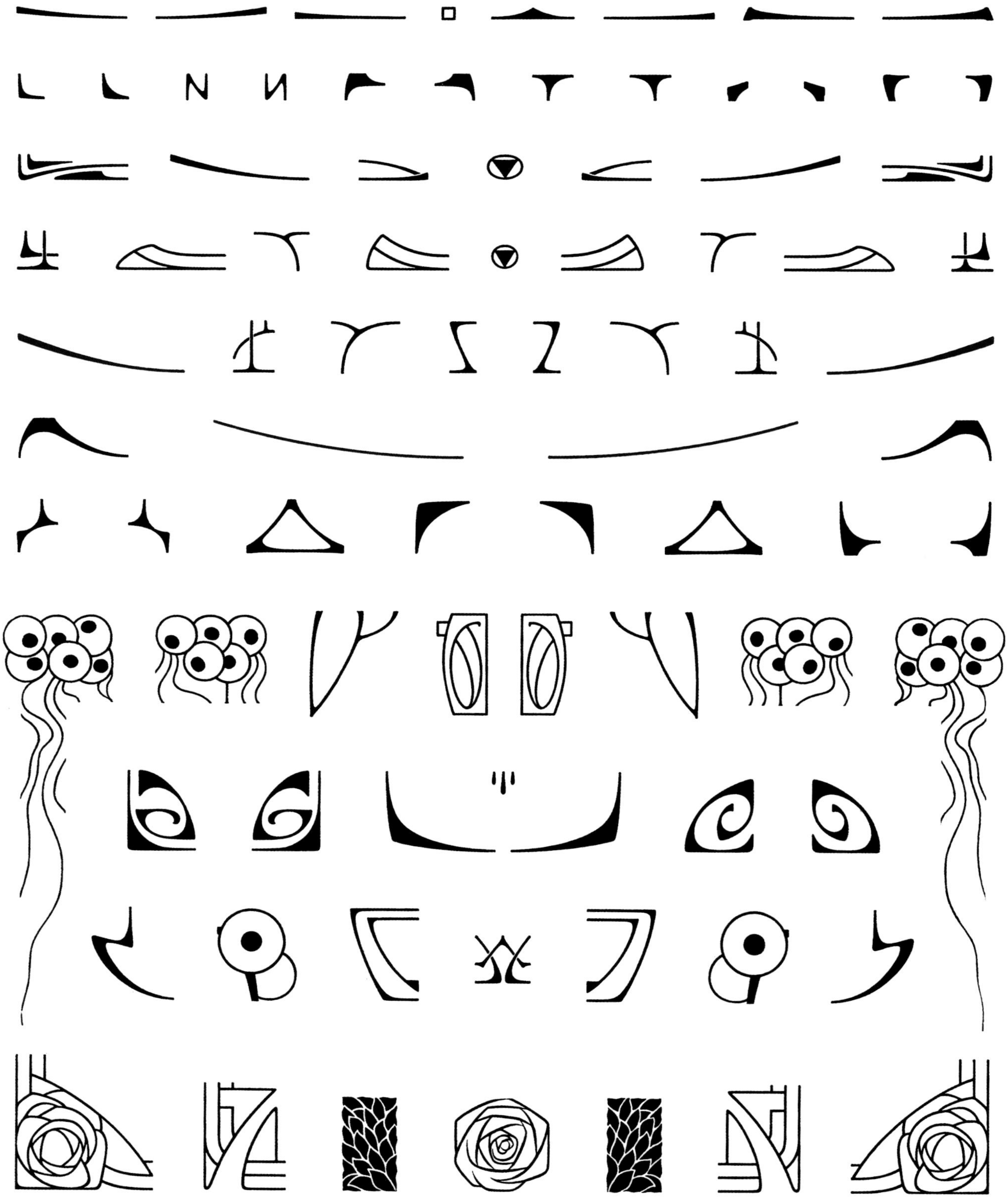

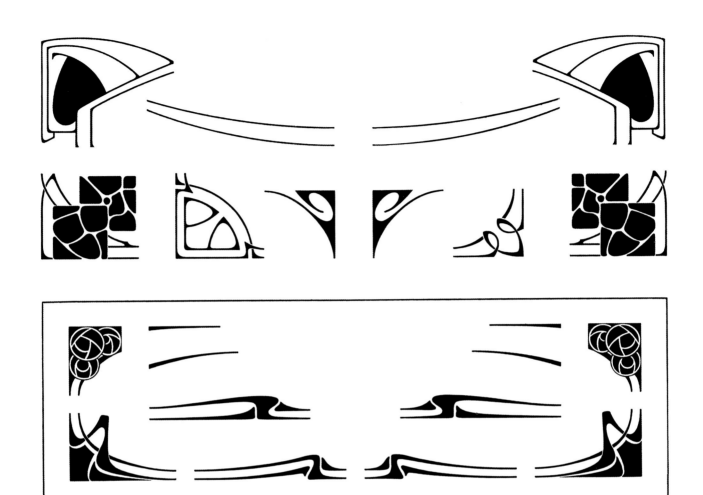

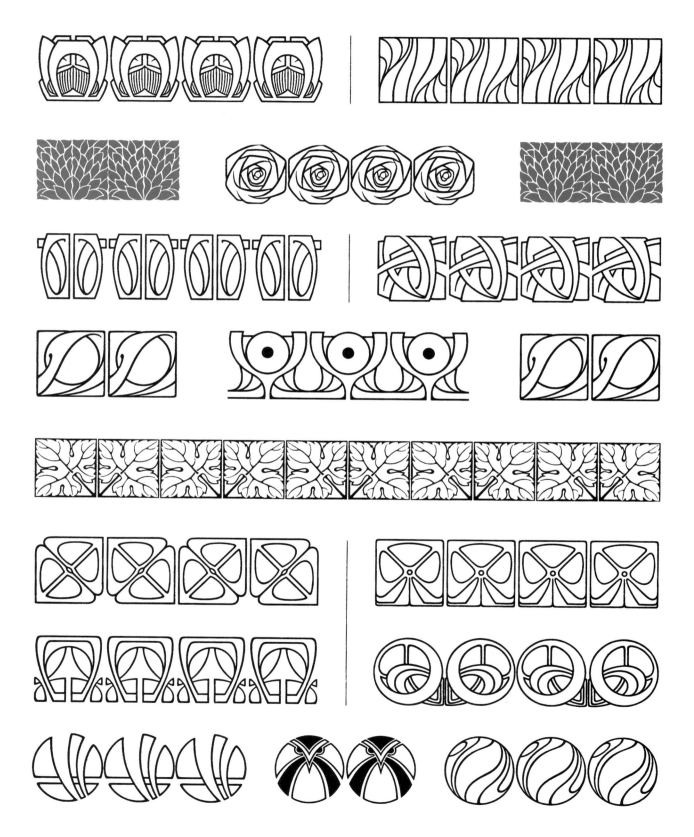

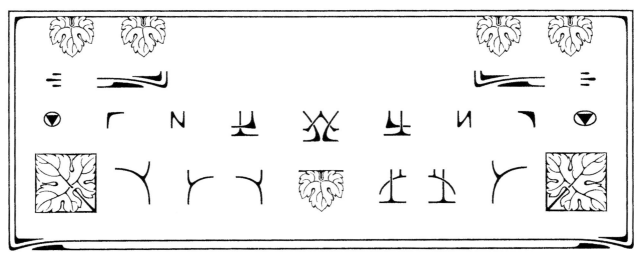

WEINE
ERSTER HÄUSER

KÜCHE
ERSTEN RANGES

HOTEL KOCH BASEL
IN GESUNDER LAGE, MIT SCHÖNER FERNSICHT
WEITERE SPAZIERGÄNGE IN NAHER WALDUNG
MIT ALLEM KOMFORT DER NEUZEIT VERSEHEN

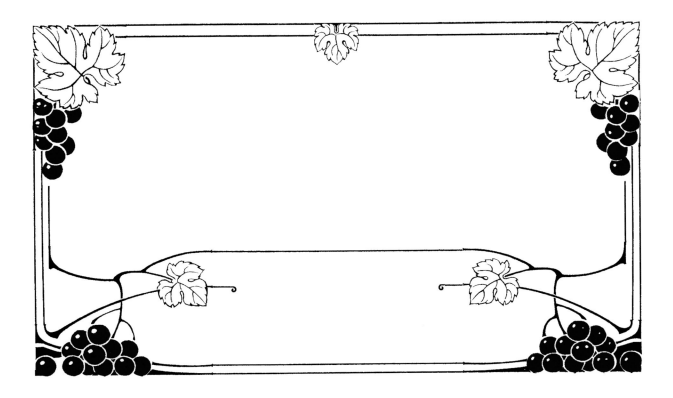

VINS

CAP MUSCATEL
BEAUNE

XERES, ST. JULIEN

CHAMPAGNER
DE ROI

VERMOUTH

COGNAC VIEUX

MENU

POTAGE À LA
CONDÉ

TURBOT SAUCE
AUX CAPRES

SALADE

HORS-D'OEUVRE

FROMAGES

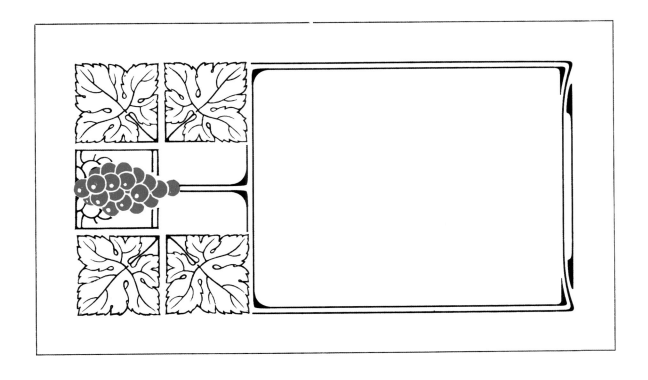

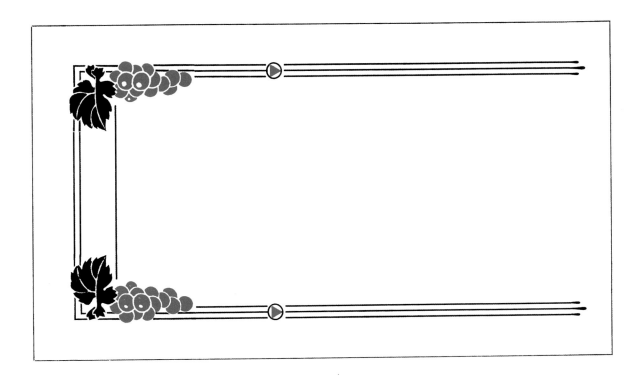

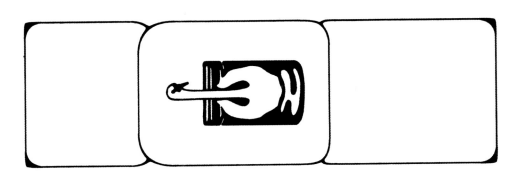

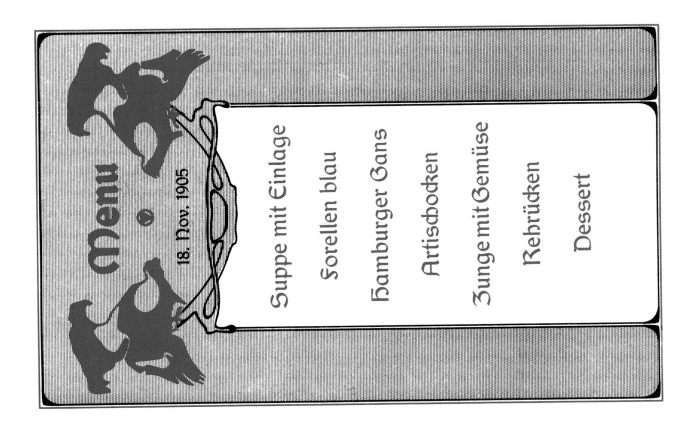

Menu

18. Nov. 1905

Suppe mit Einlage

Forellen blau

Hamburger Gans

Artischocken

Zunge mit Gemüse

Rehrücken

Dessert

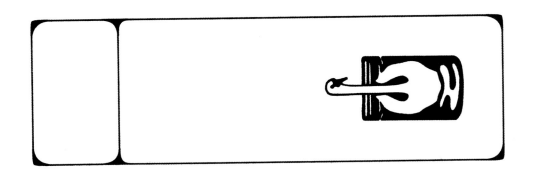

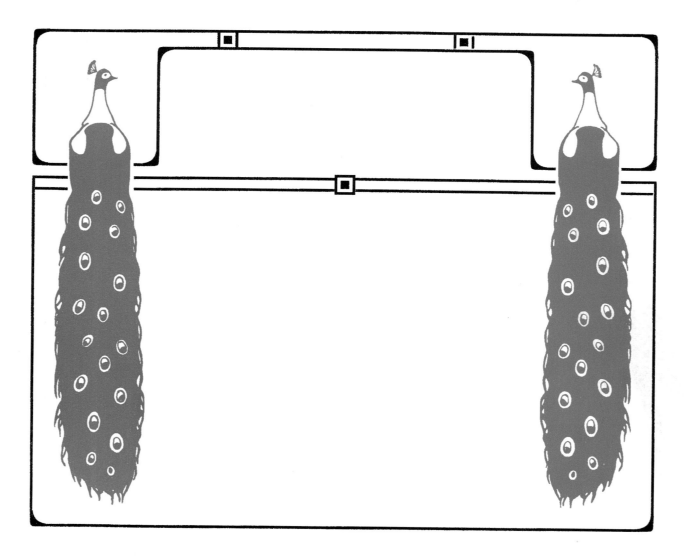

Taken from **The Decoupage Sourcebook** by Jocasta Innes and Stewart Walton
(£12.99, Conran Octopus). Available at all good bookshops.

HOTEL ZUM SCHWANEN
SPEISEKARTE

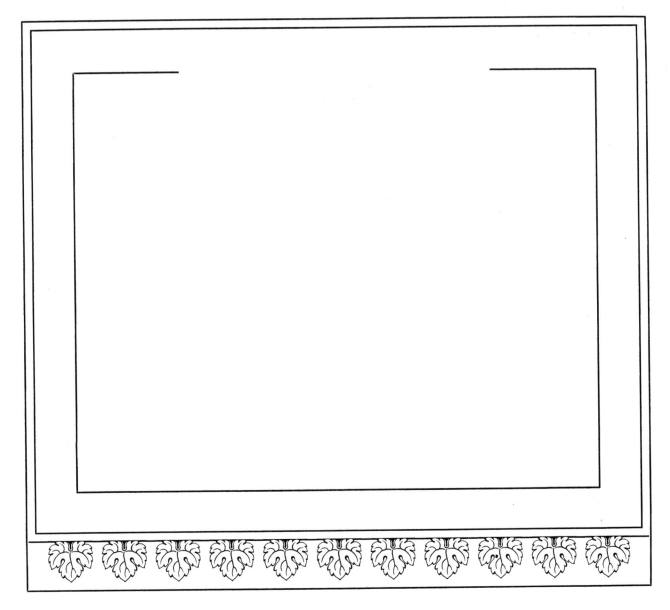

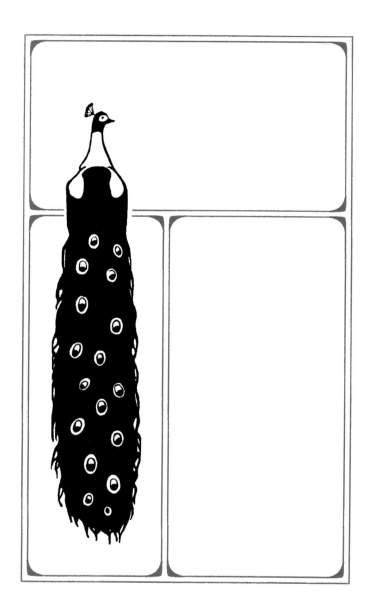

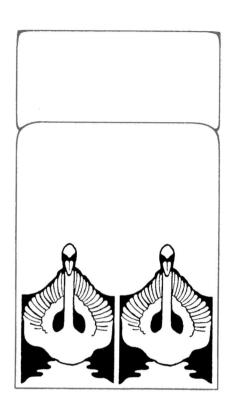

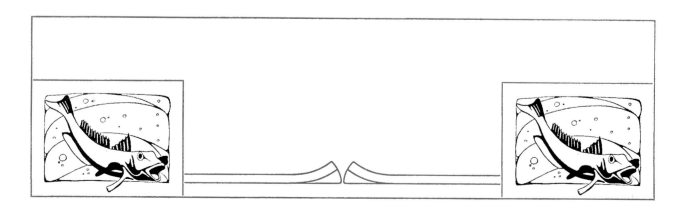

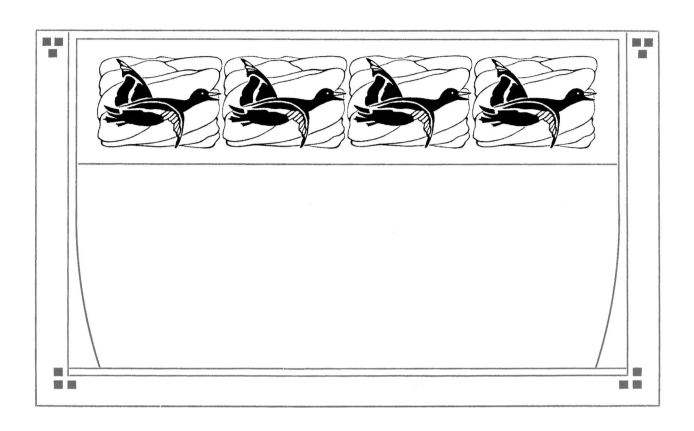

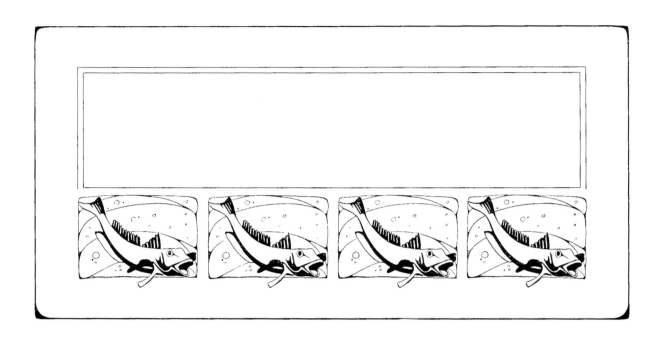

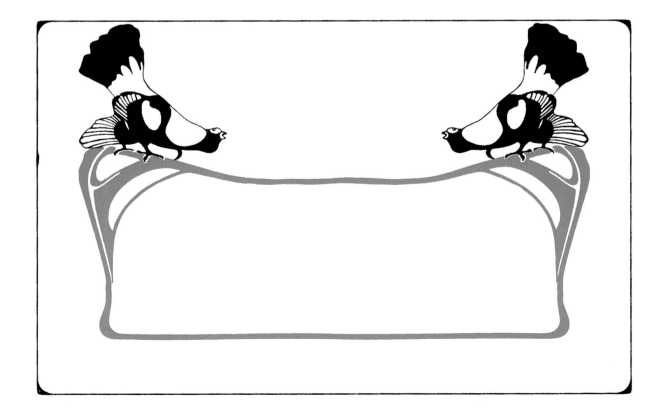

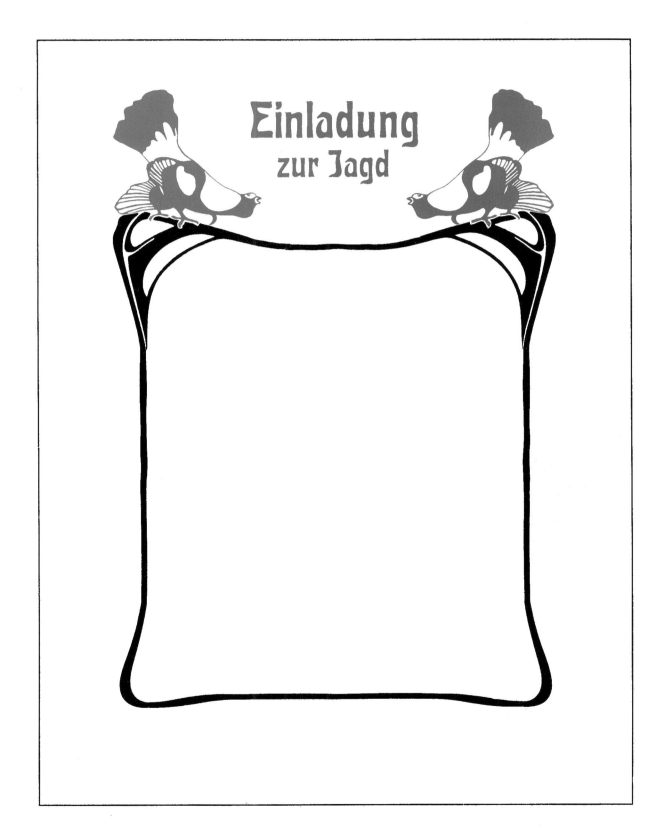

Einladung
zur Jagd

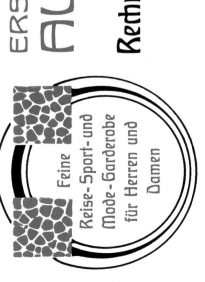

ERSTES KÖLNER MODEHAUS
AUGUST QUACK

Feine
Reise-Sport- und
Mode-Garderobe
für Herren und
Damen

Rechnung für

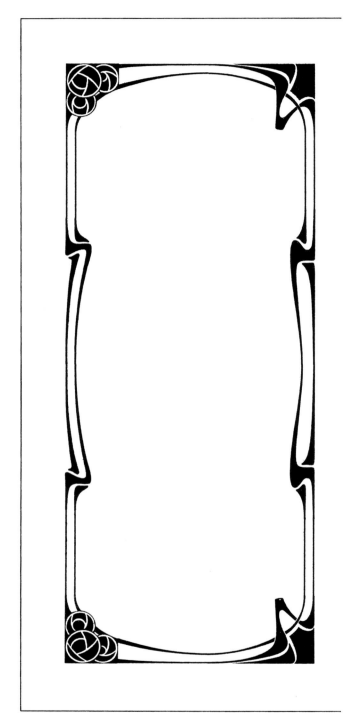

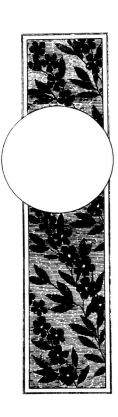

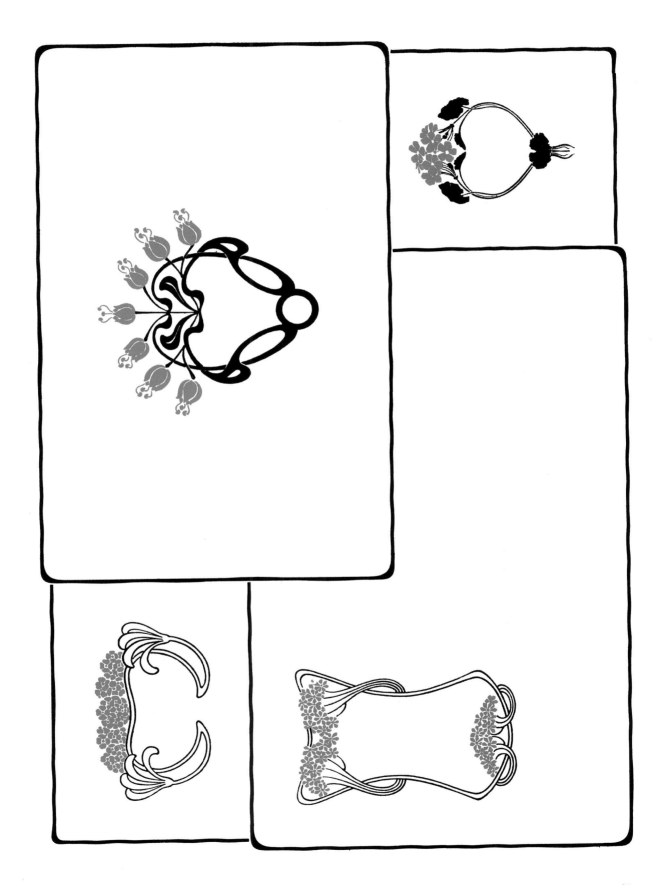

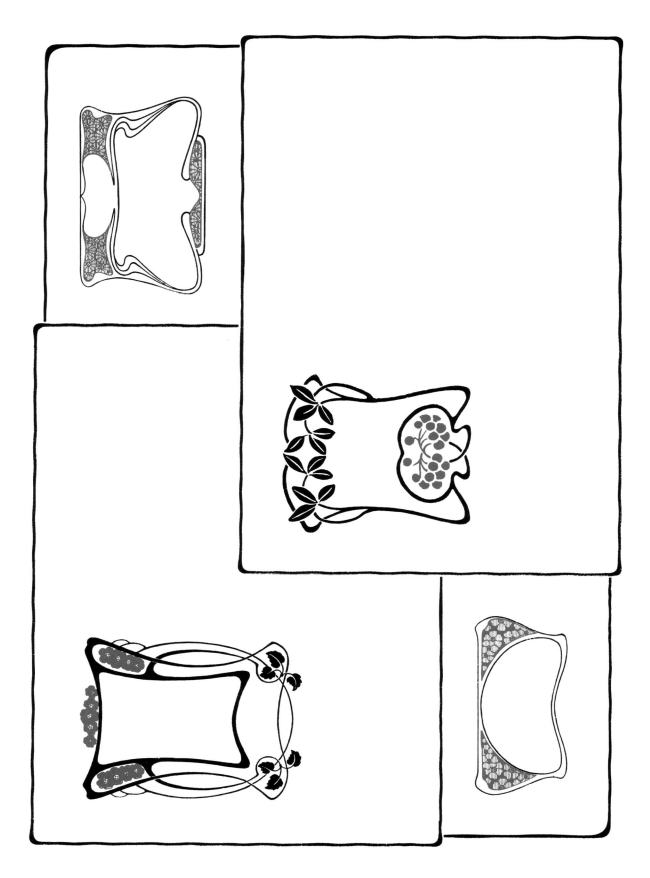

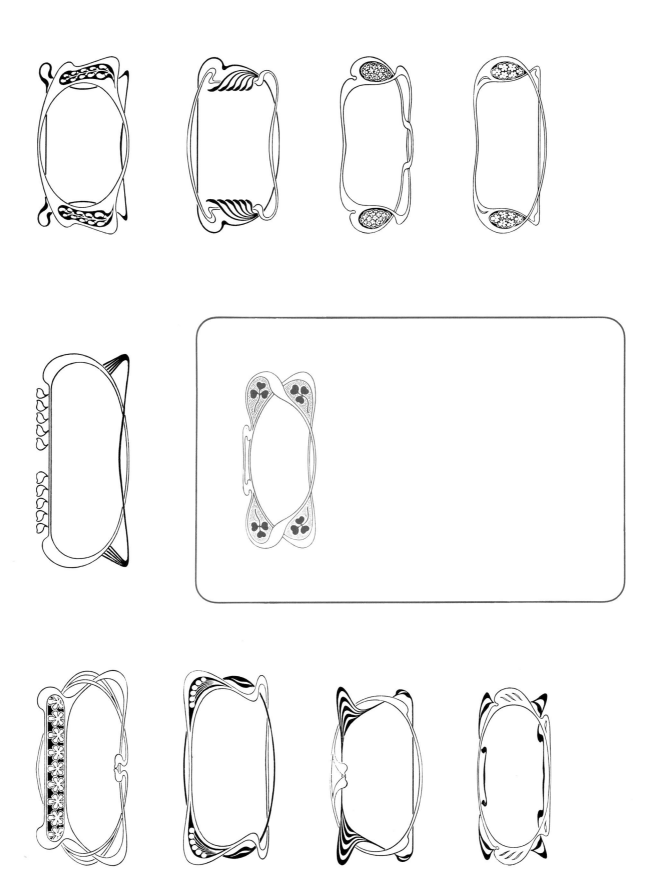

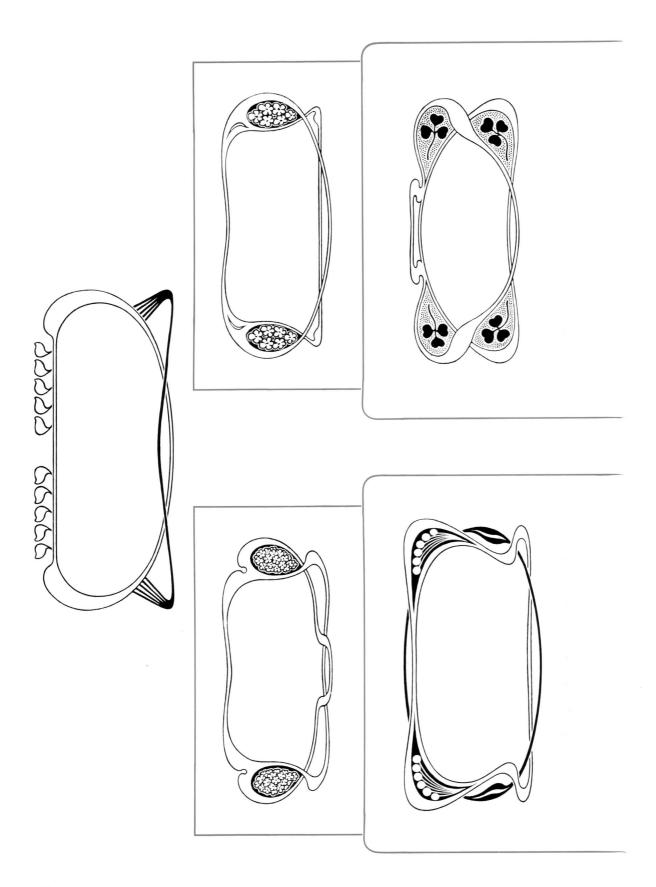

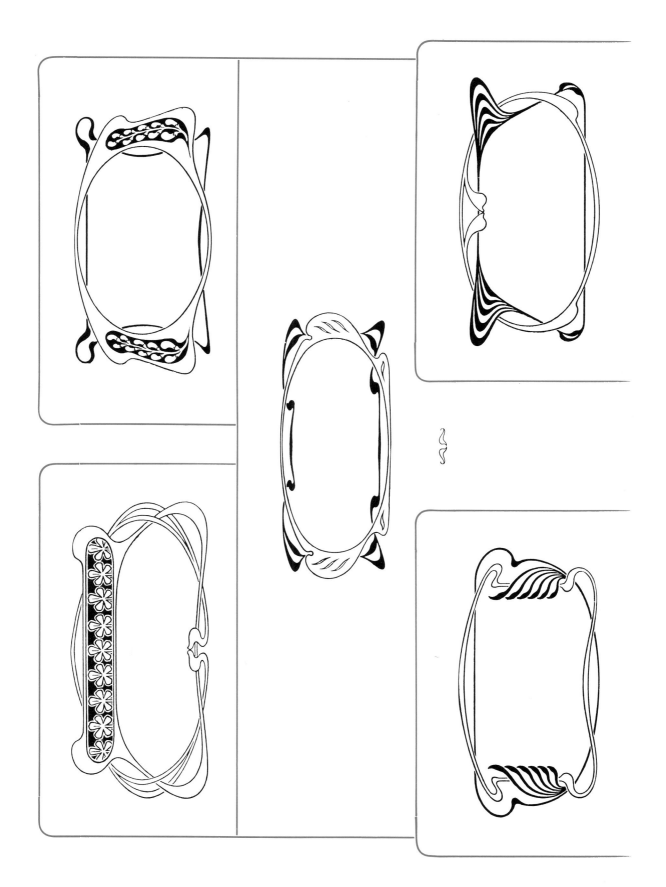

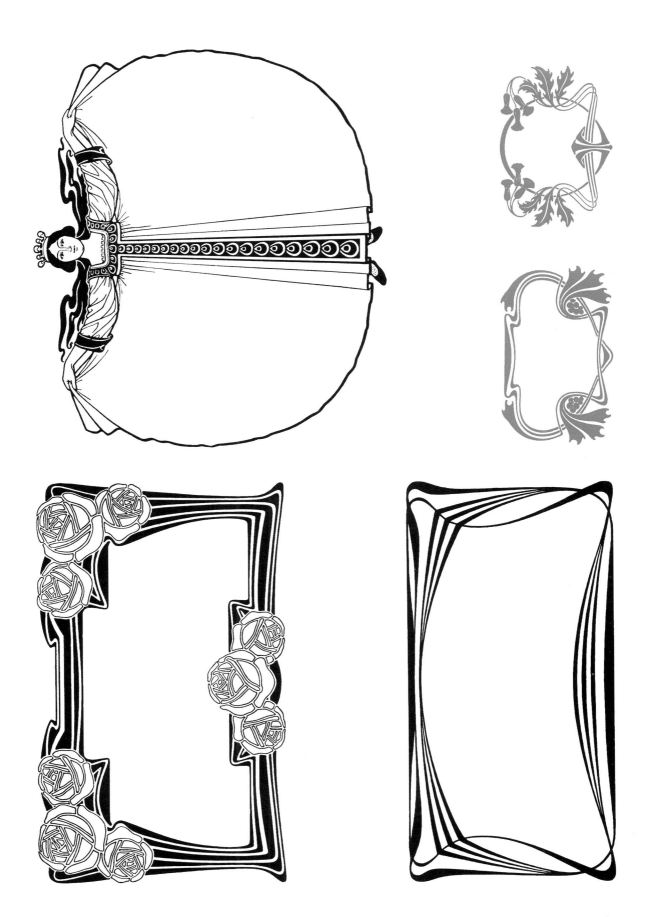

Christmas Greetings

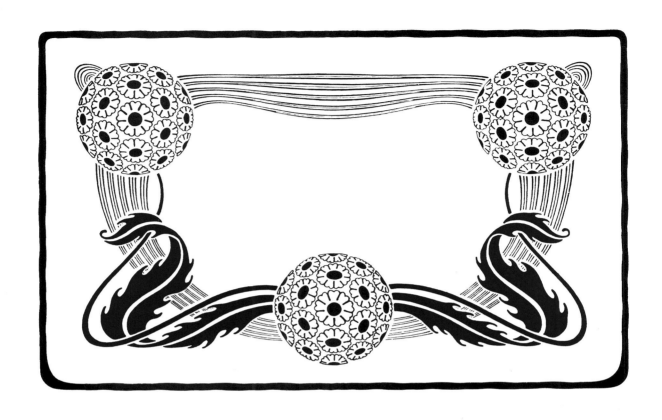

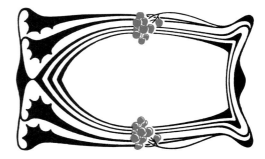

Aan=
kondiging

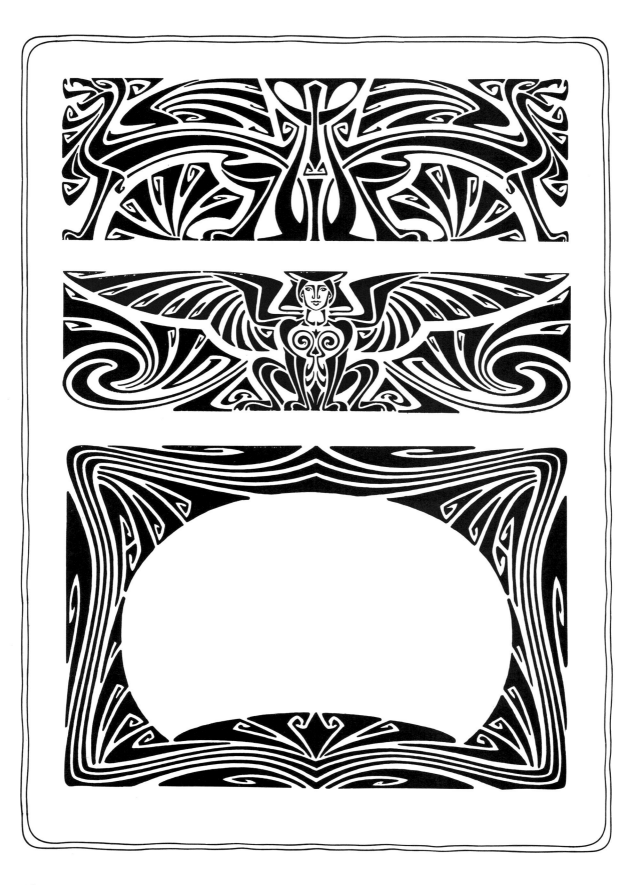

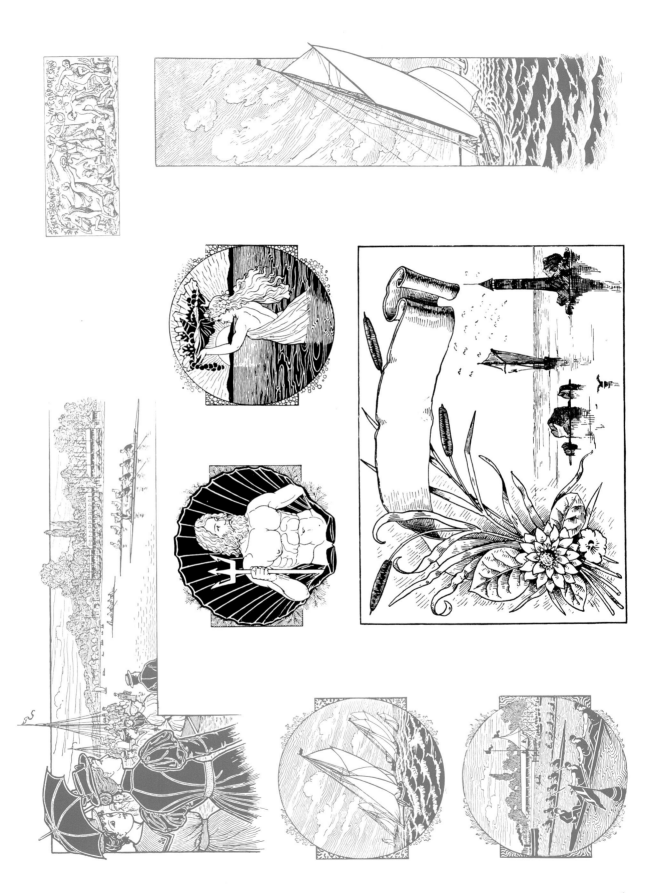

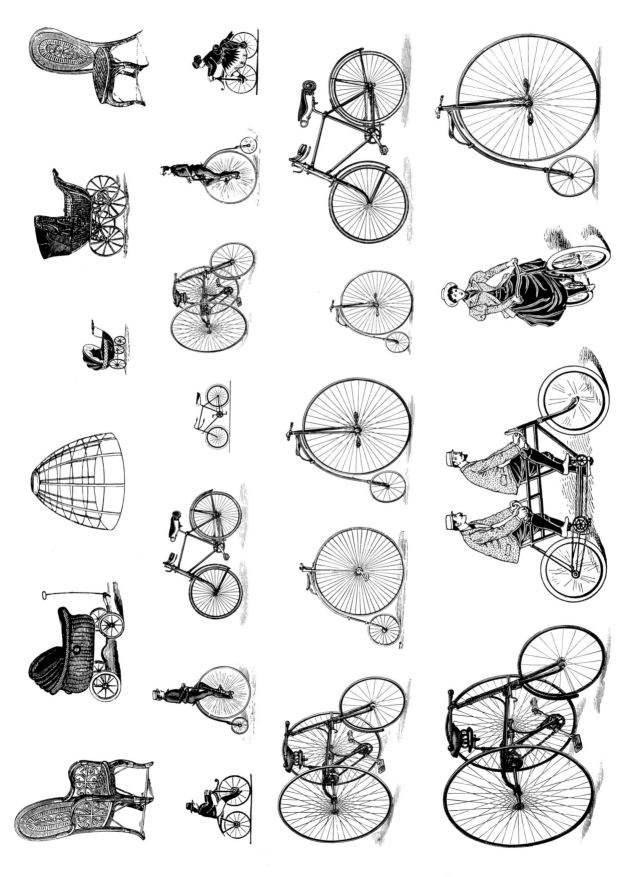

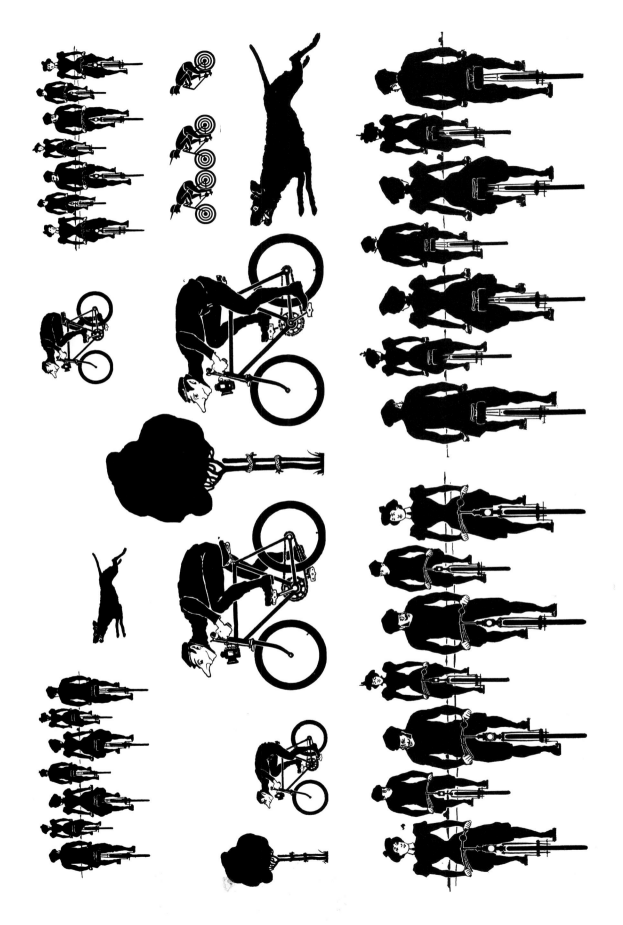

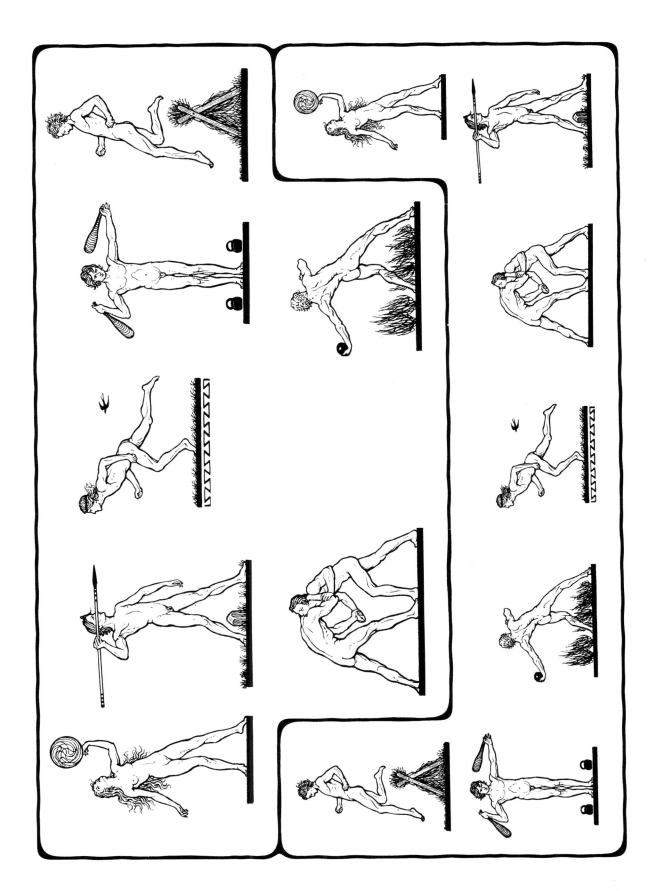

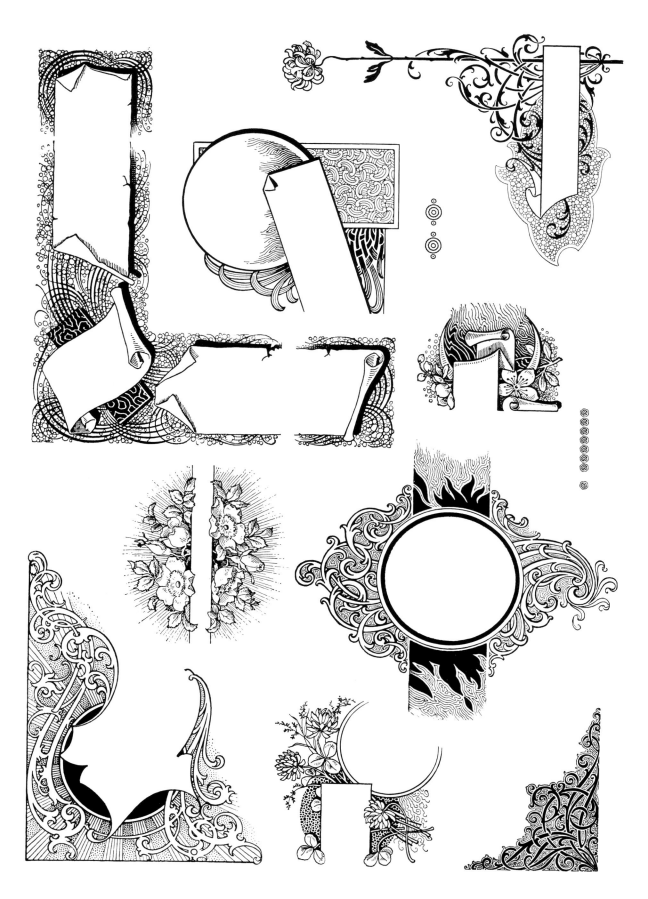

MY
CHRISTMAS
WISH

May you be blest
With all that
earth
can lend
Long life,
Good health
True pleasures
and a friend

A HAPPY NEW YEAR

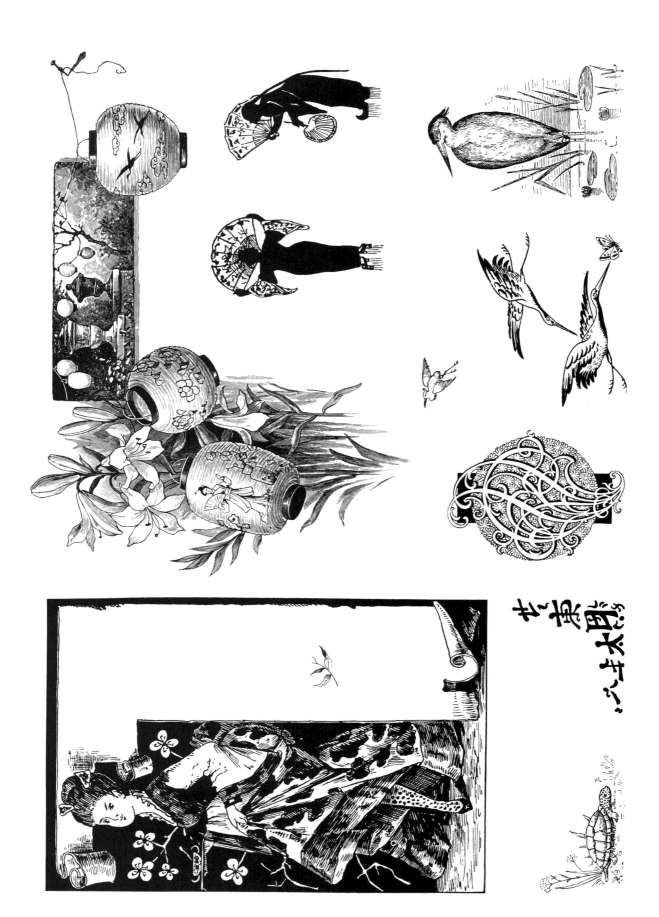

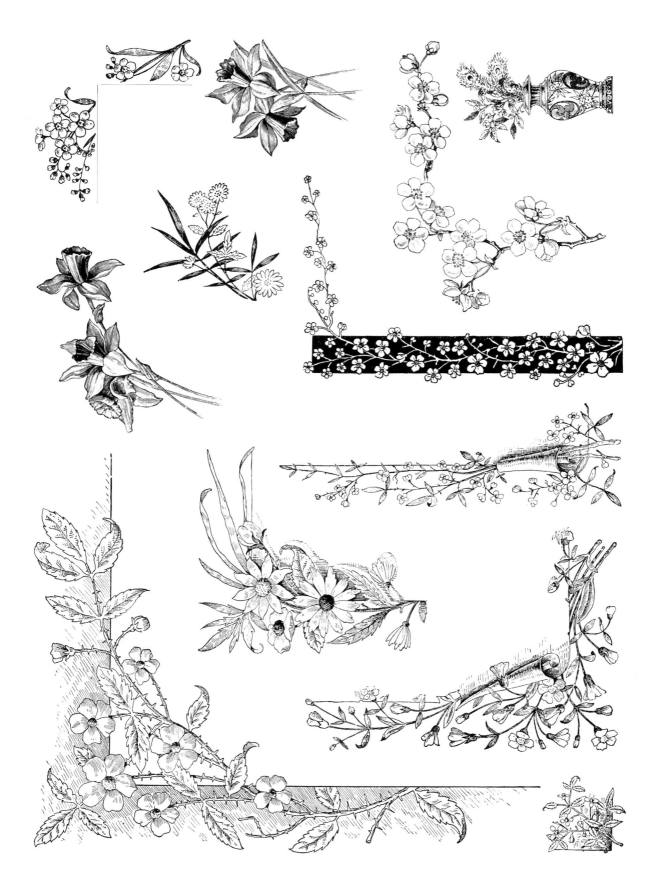

Von

Sansibar

zum

Tanganjika

Briefe aus Ostafrika

von

Dr. Heinrich Burger

Gymnasialdirektor

zu Neustadt

2. Auflage

Preis 6 Mark

Hamburg

Verlag der Hölze'schen Buchhandlung

1896

Naturgeschichtliches
VOLKSLEXIKON

20 Bände
mit Supplementen
in 5 Bänden

von

Ferdinand von Sternburg

Zweiter Band

Stuttgart * München
Druck und Verlag von Wilhelm Lions Erben
1896

Konzert

VIGNETTEN

in

japanischem Charakter

für Umrandung

Ein- und
mehrfarbig

Ausschmuck

und

Unterdruck

Feinstes
Brief-Postpapier

Neuthaler Papierfabrik
Gebrüder Siebmann

HIOGO

Eine japanische Romanze

München

Verlag von Karl Elsterberg

Japanische Zierstücke

Unterdruckmuster

für Karten und andere Drucke

in japanischer

Ausstattung

VIGNETTEN

S

Menu

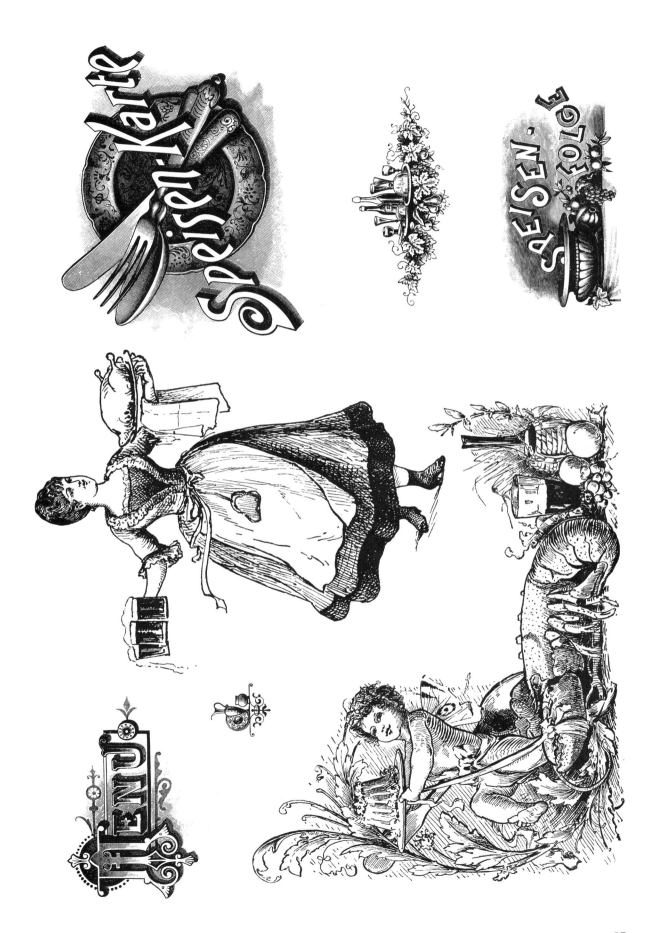

WEIN-LISTE

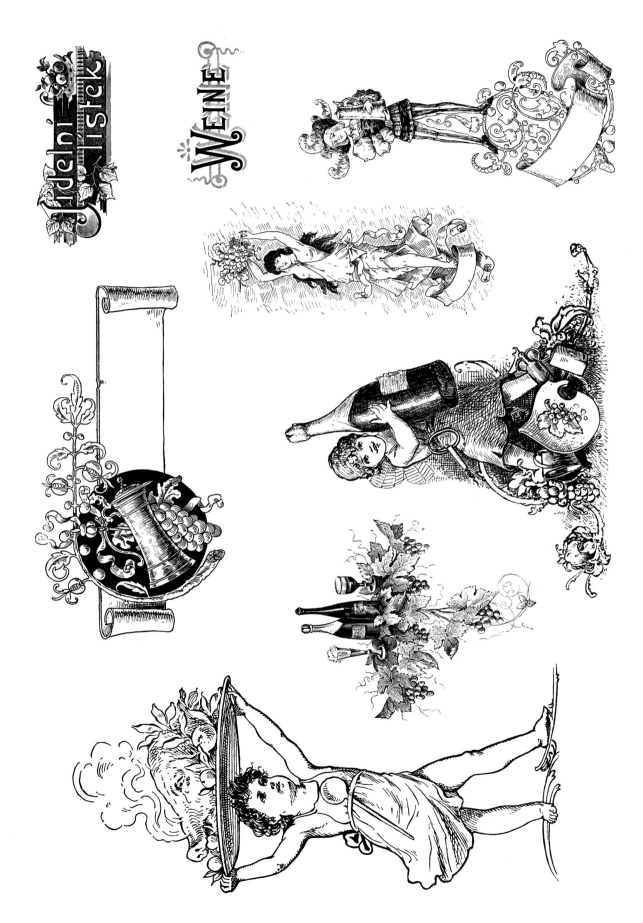

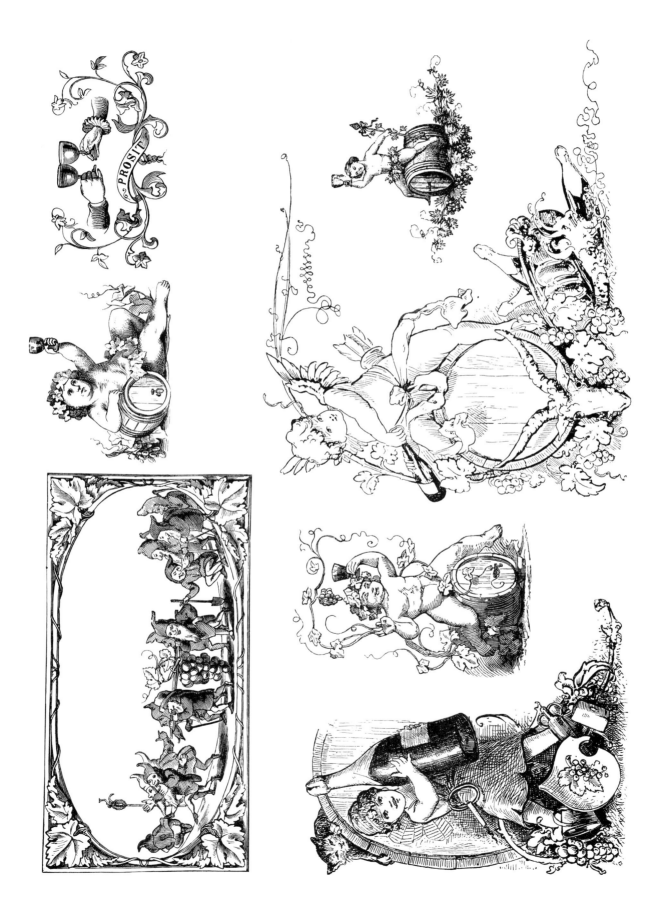

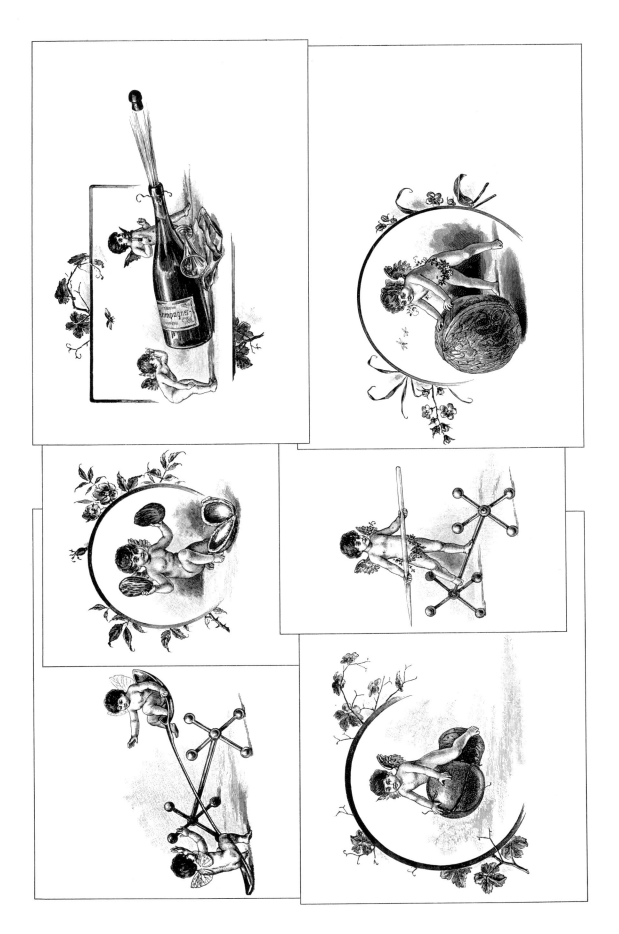

St. Julien

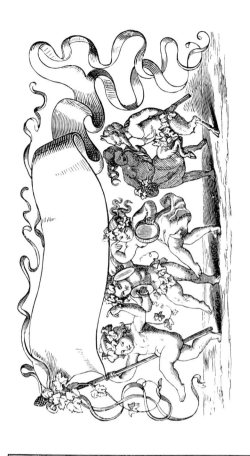

107

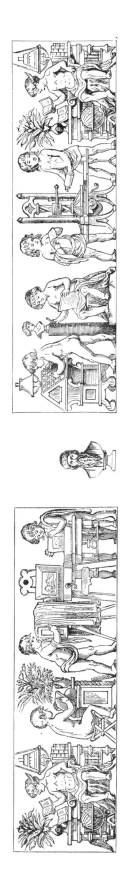

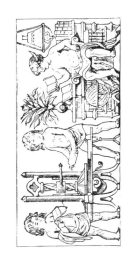

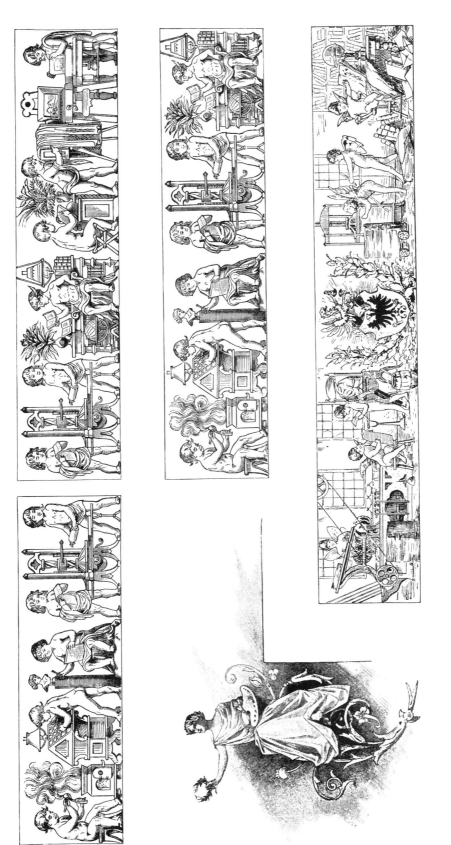

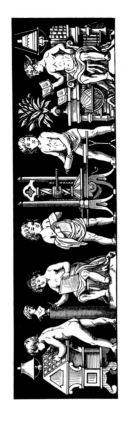

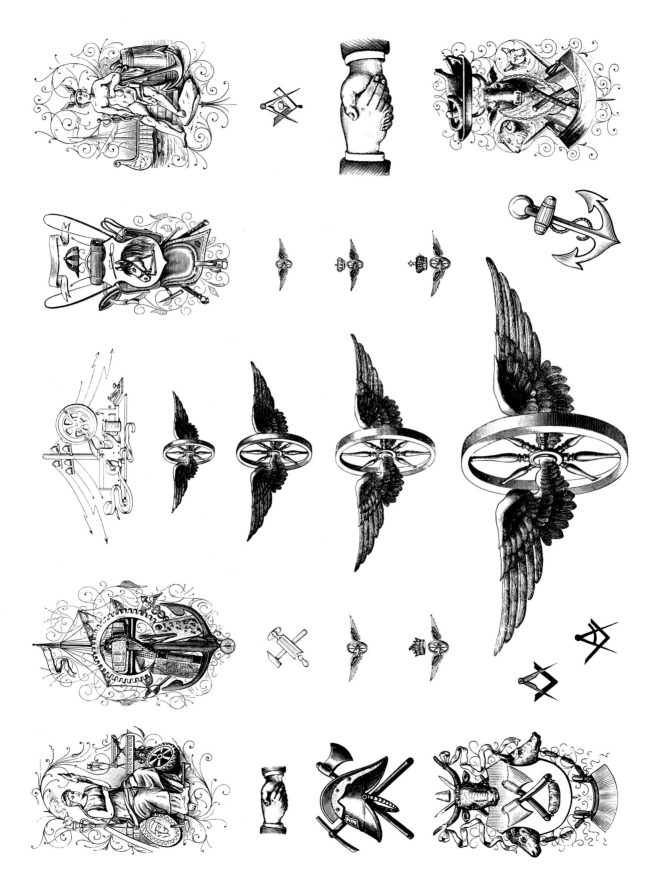

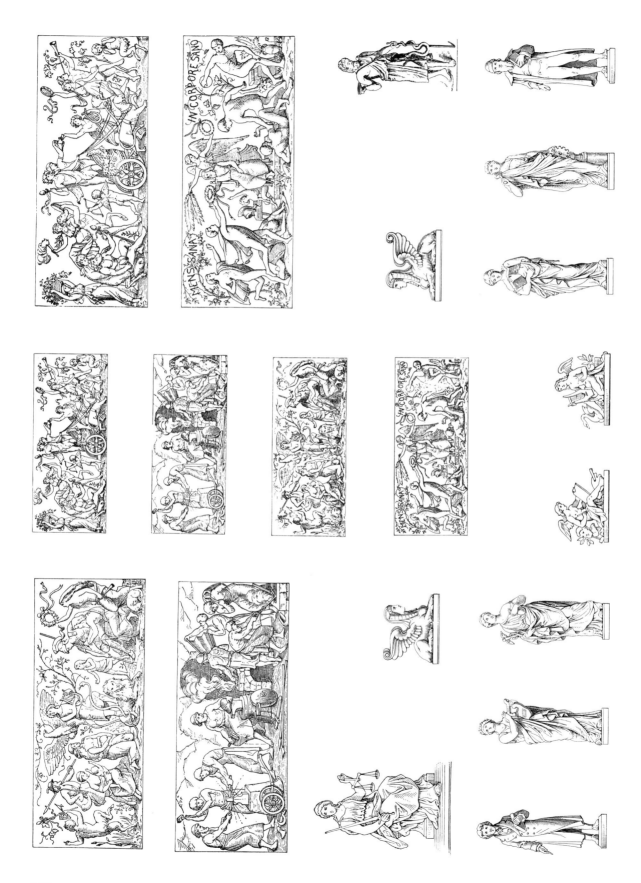

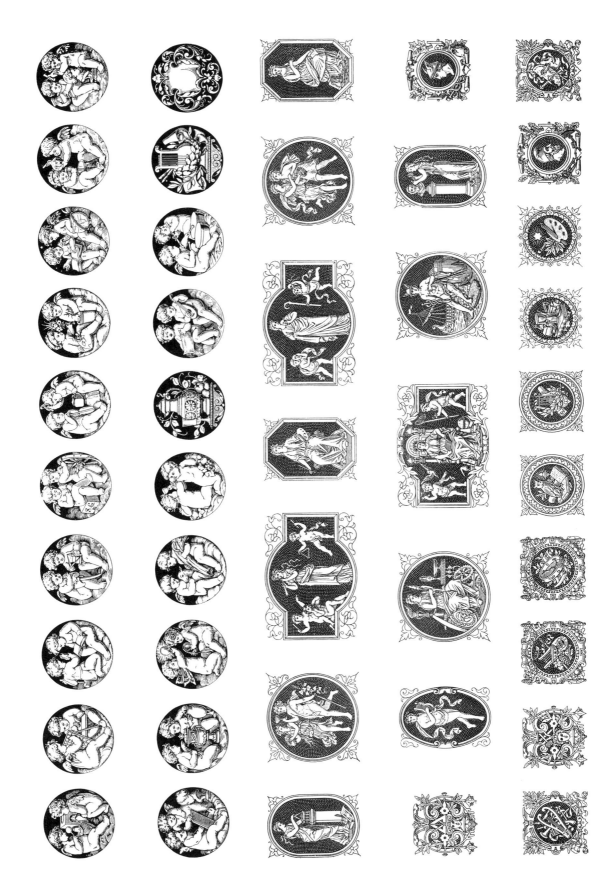

Christbaumkerzen.

Wachsstöcke.

Stearinkerzen.

Eau de Cologne & Haaröl.

Seife.

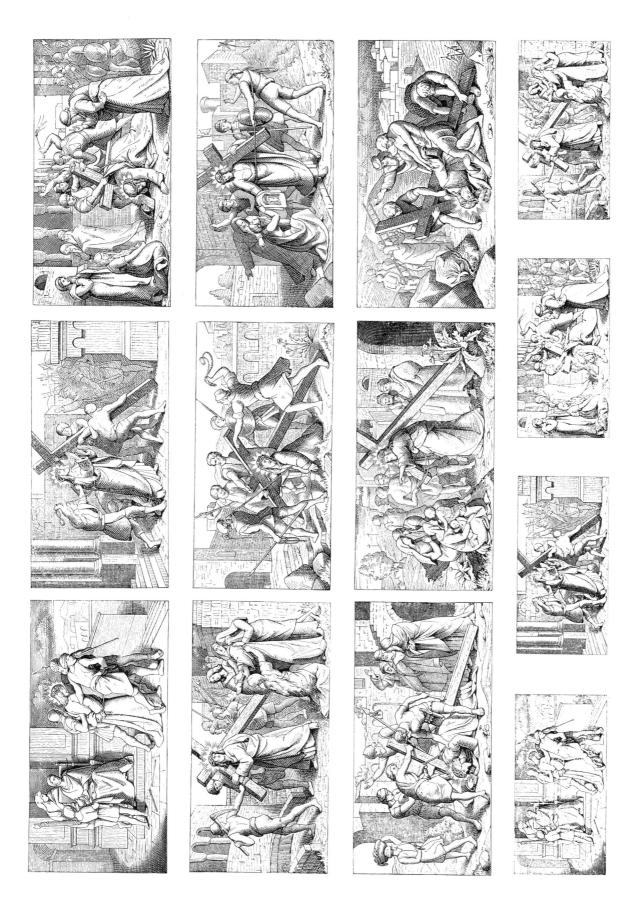

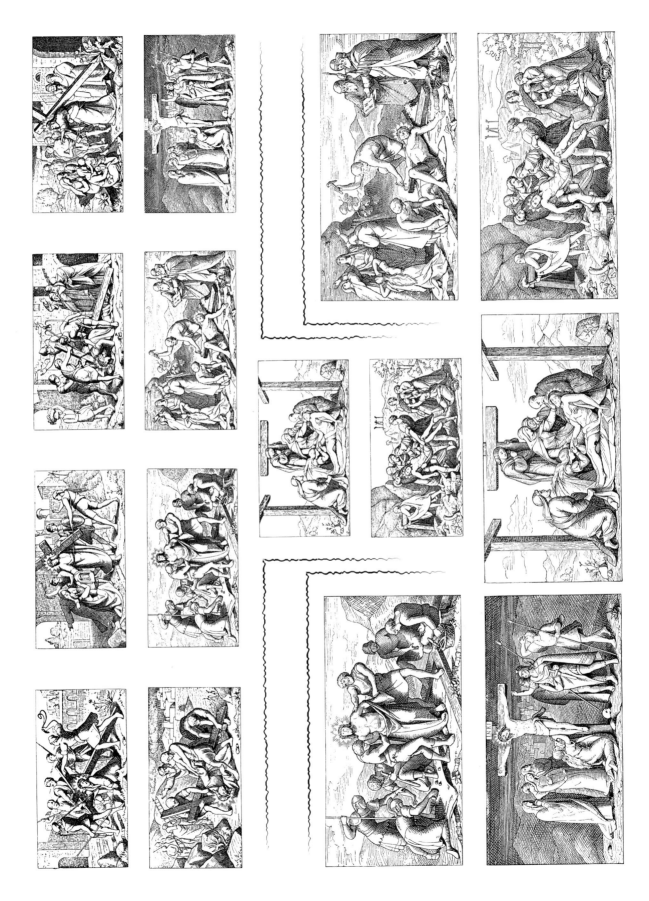

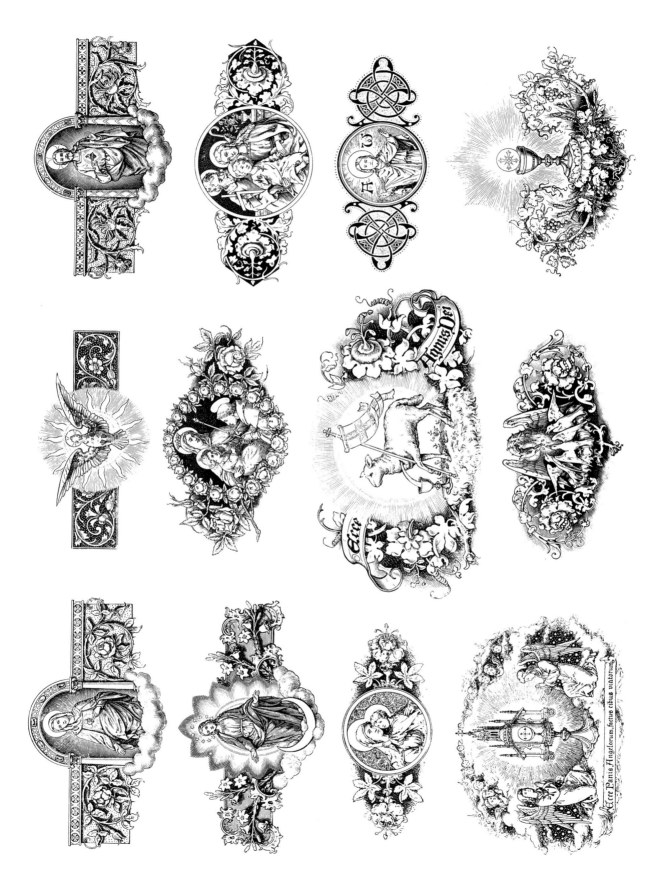

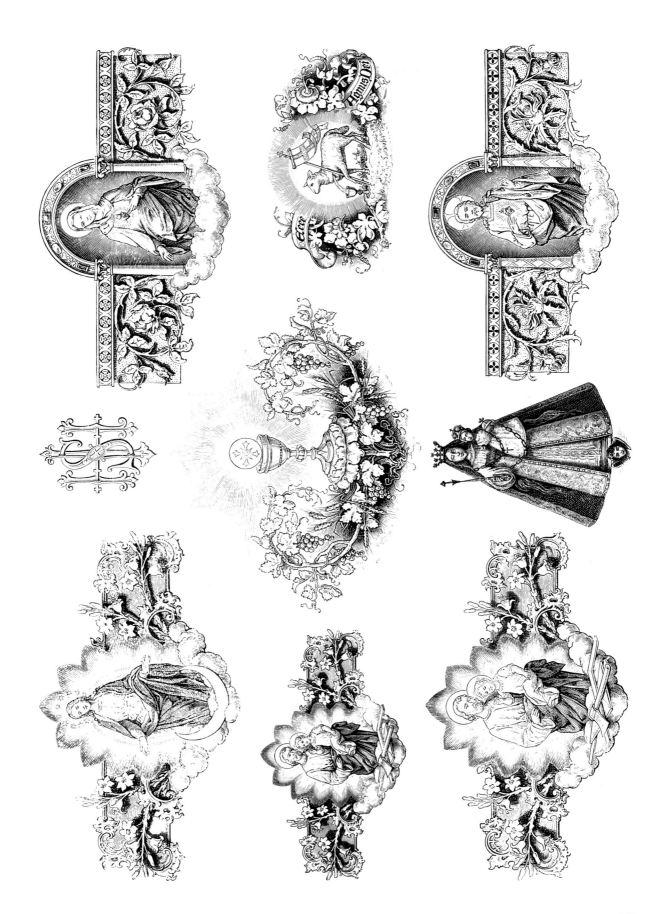

133

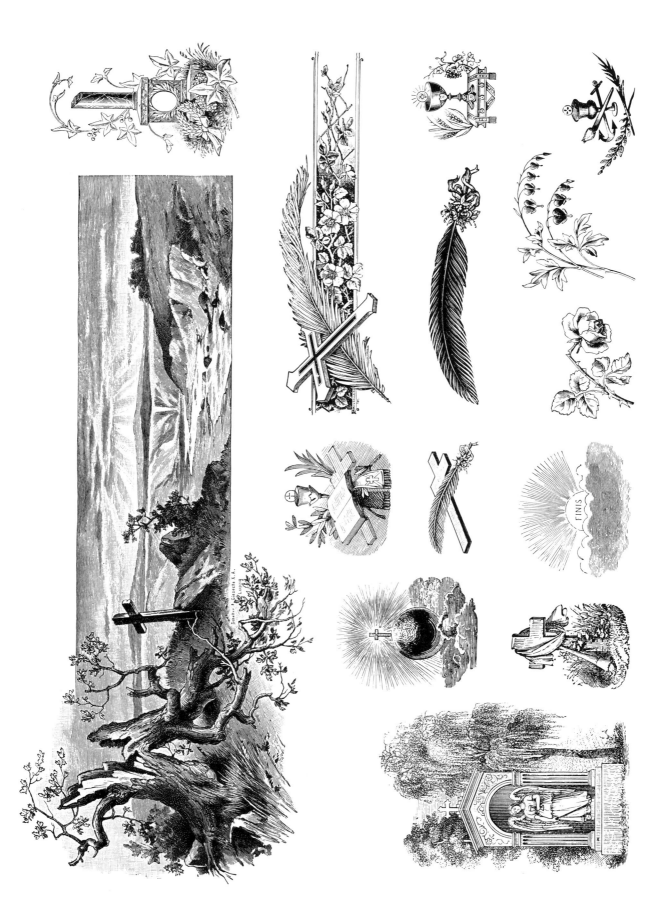

139

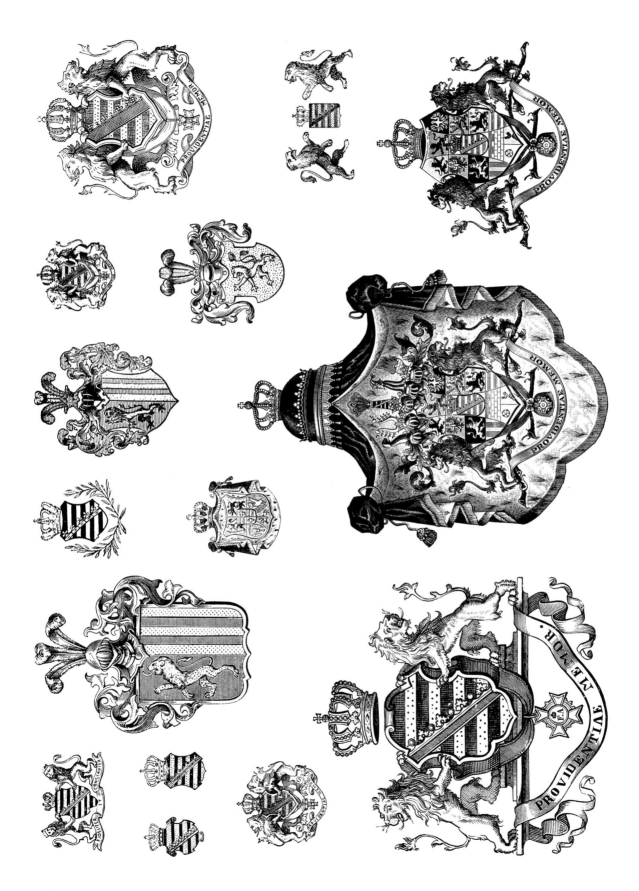

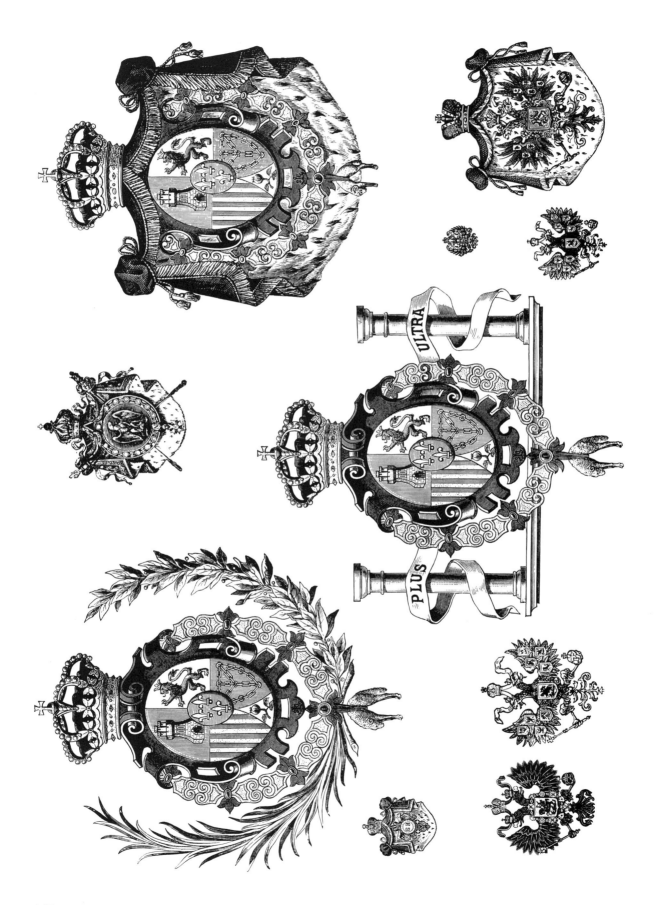

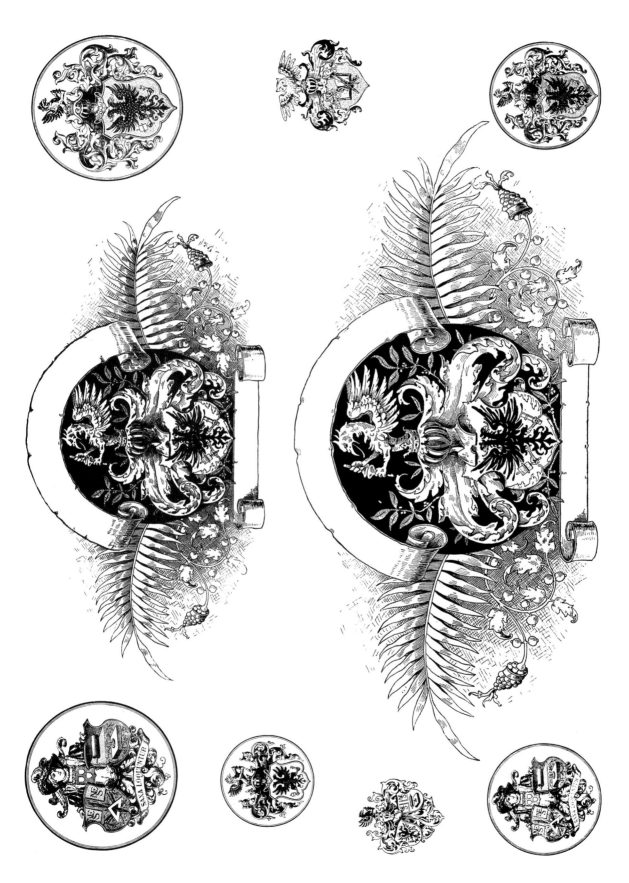

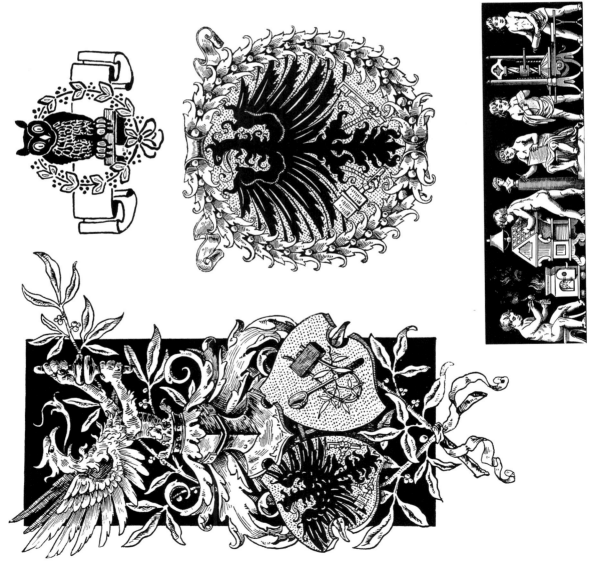

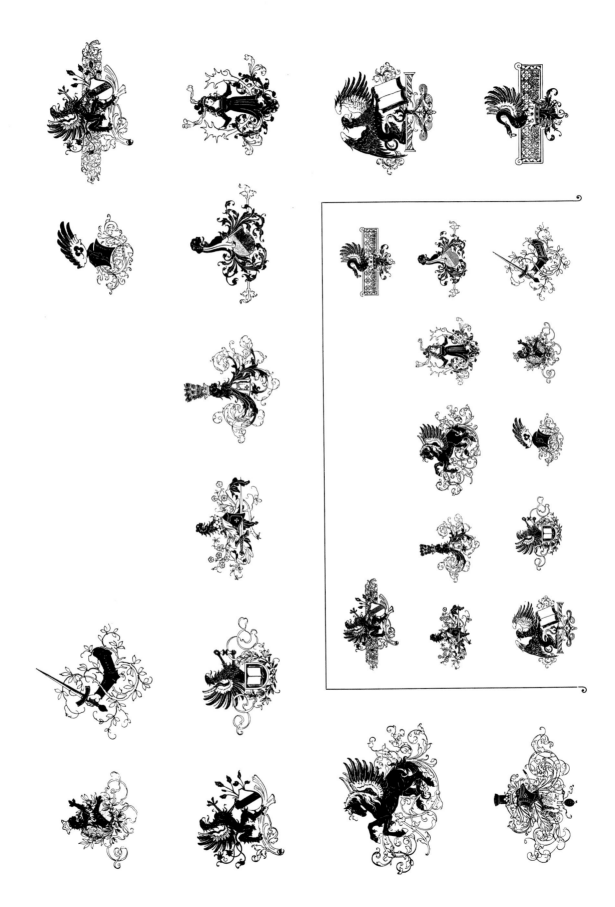

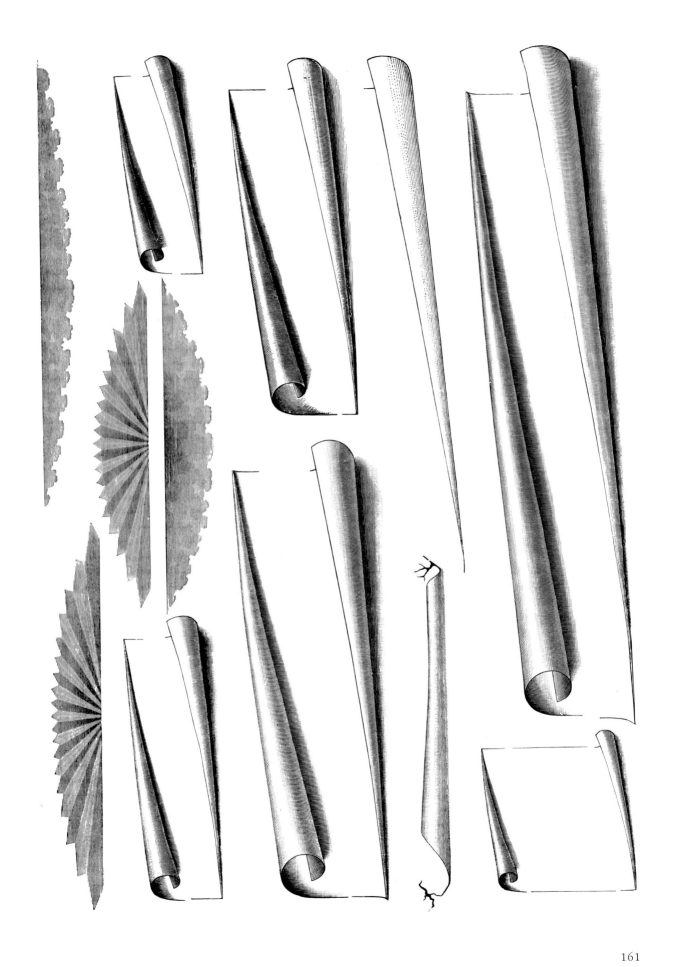

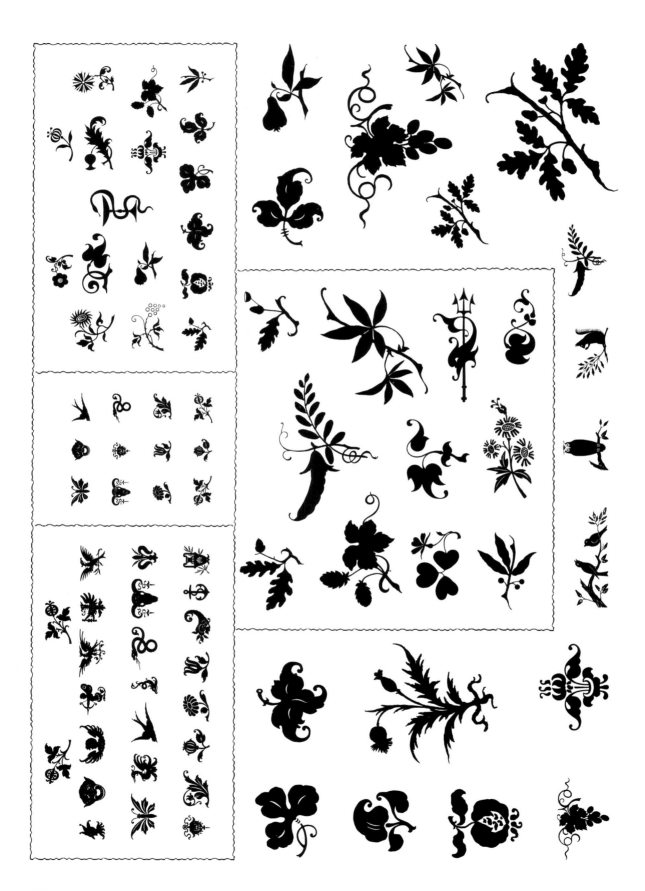

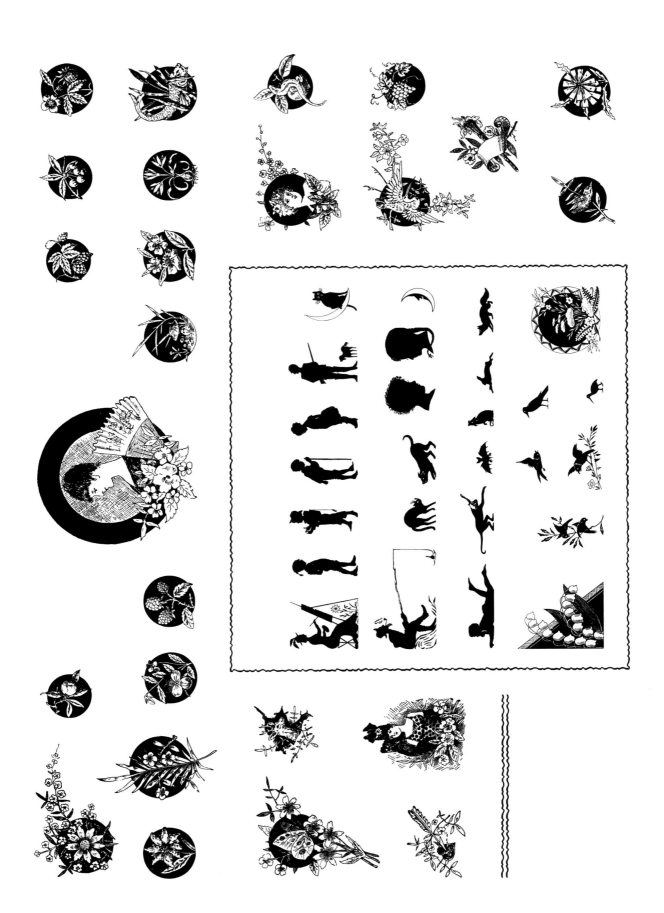

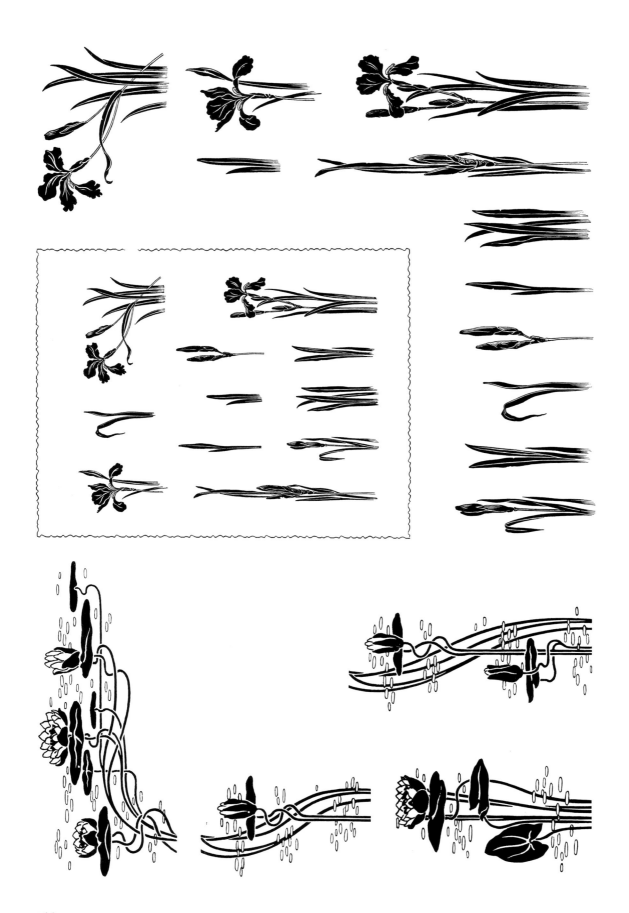

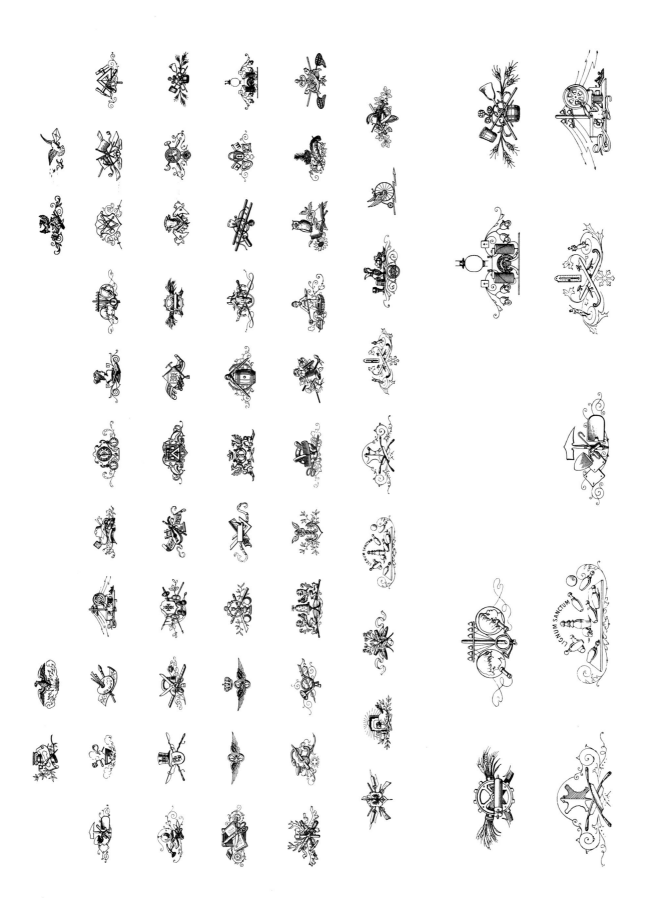

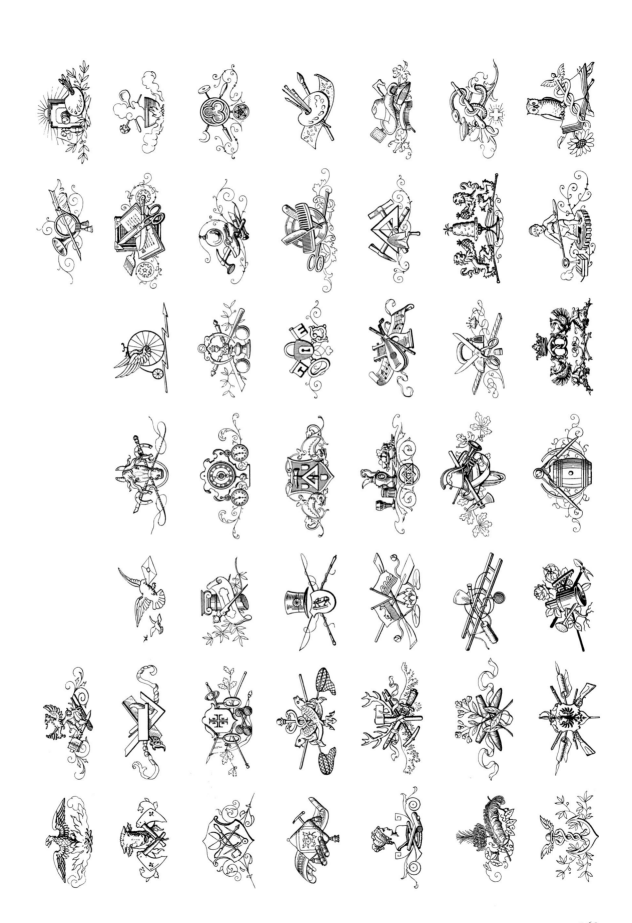

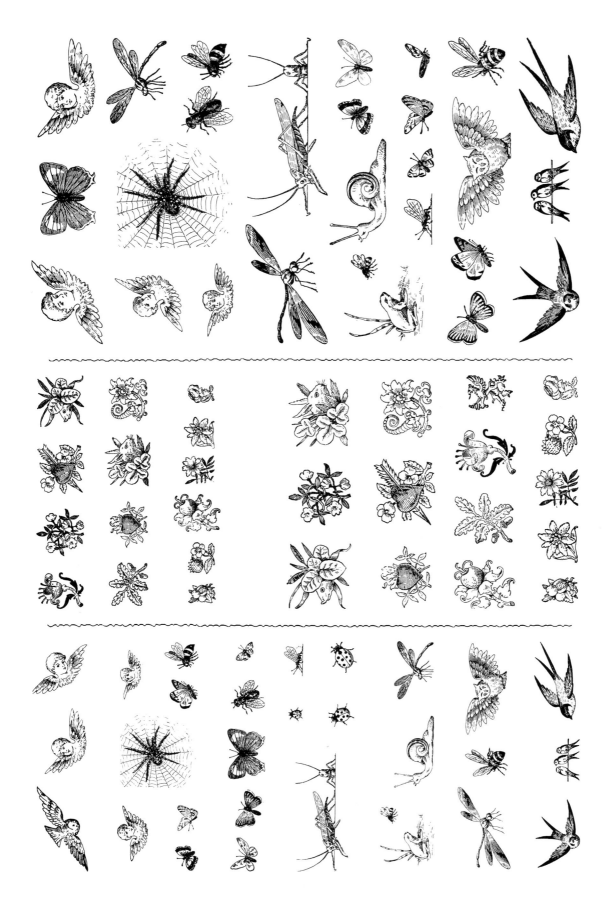

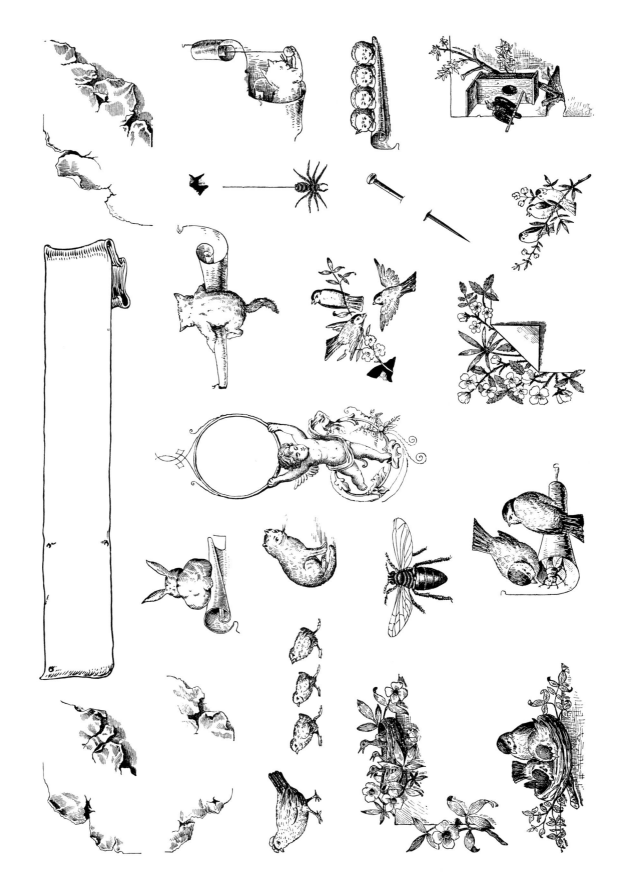

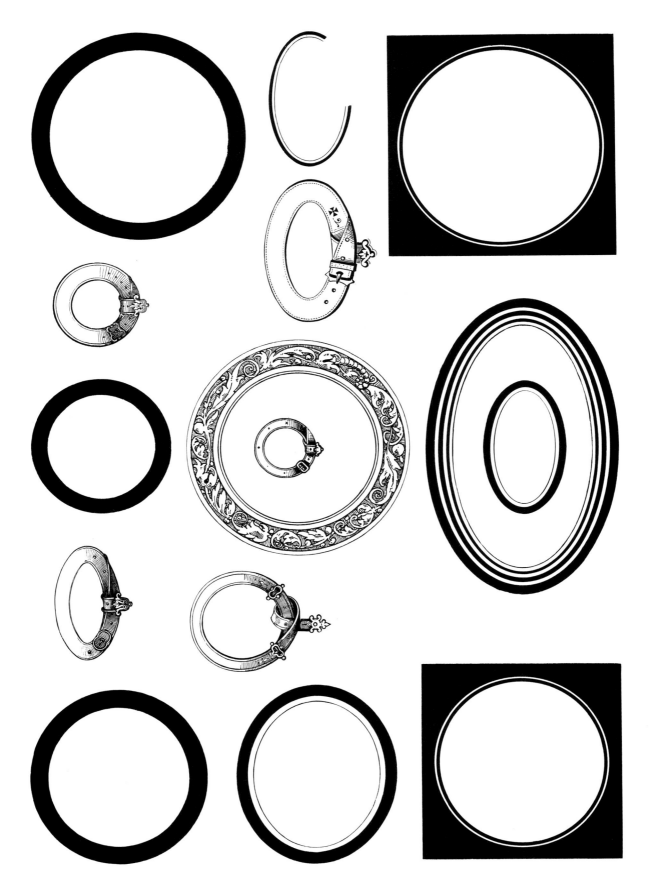

174

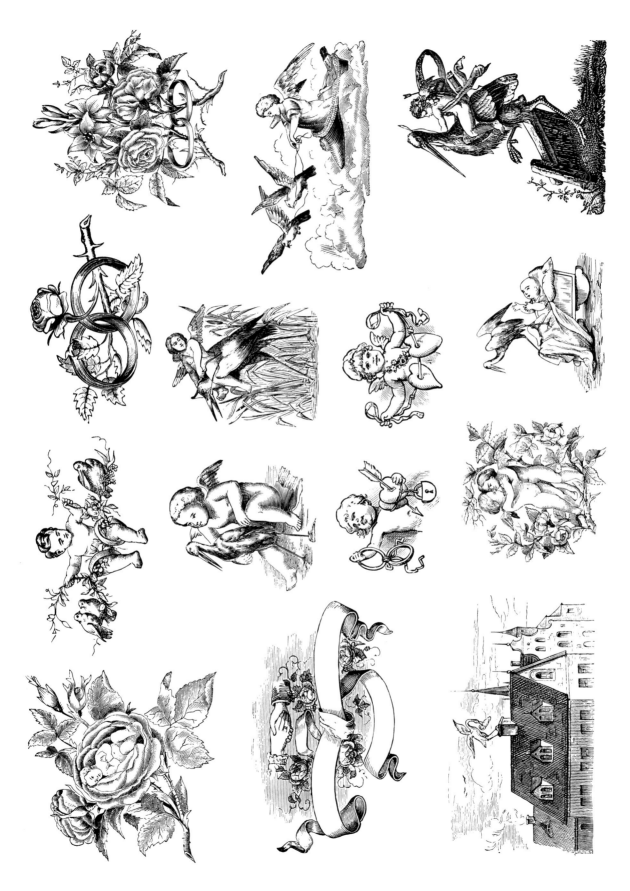

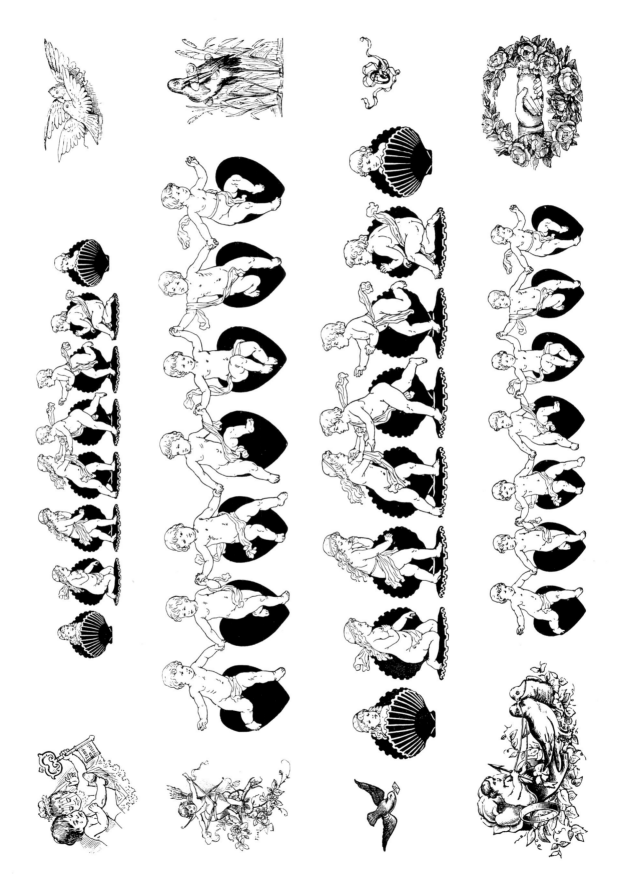

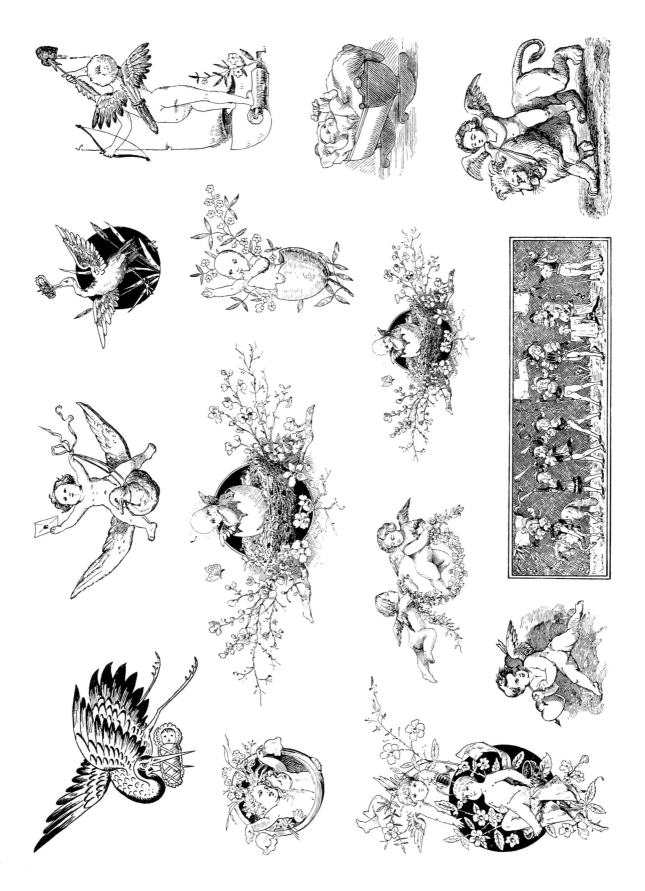

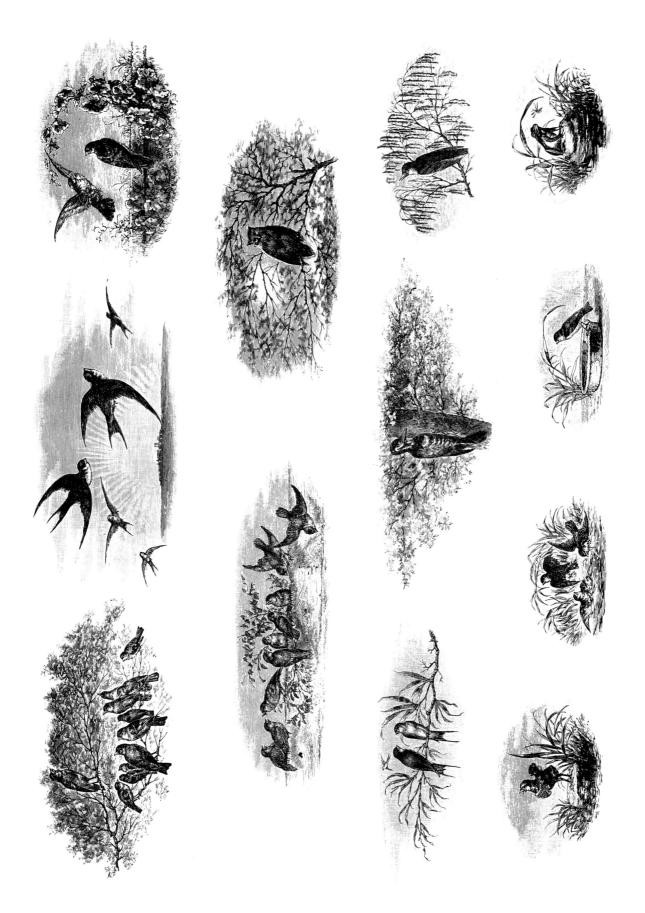

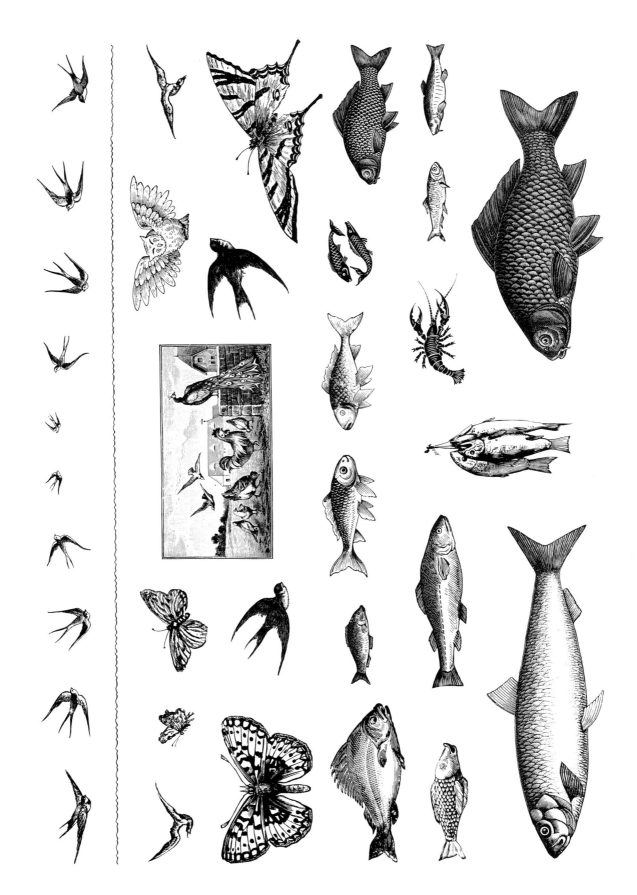

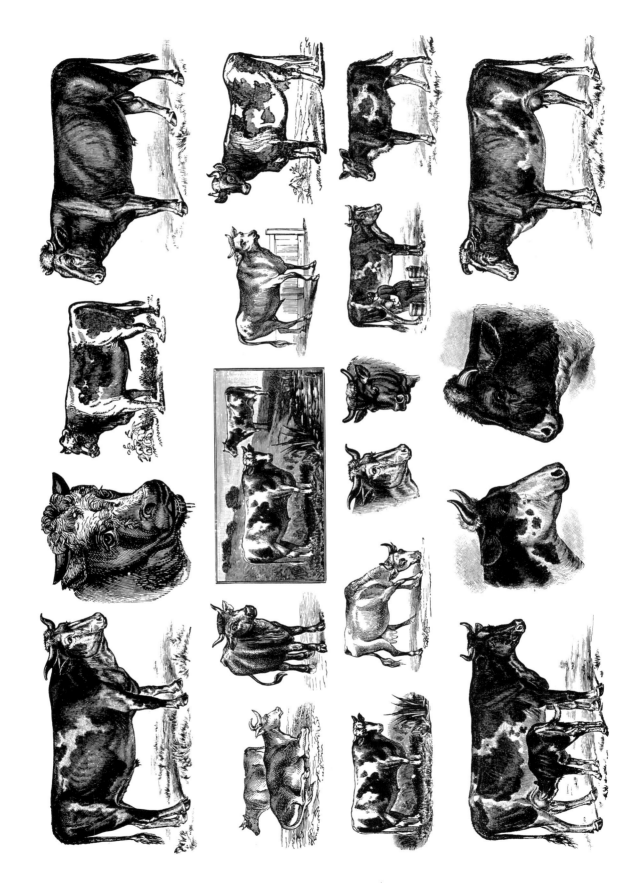

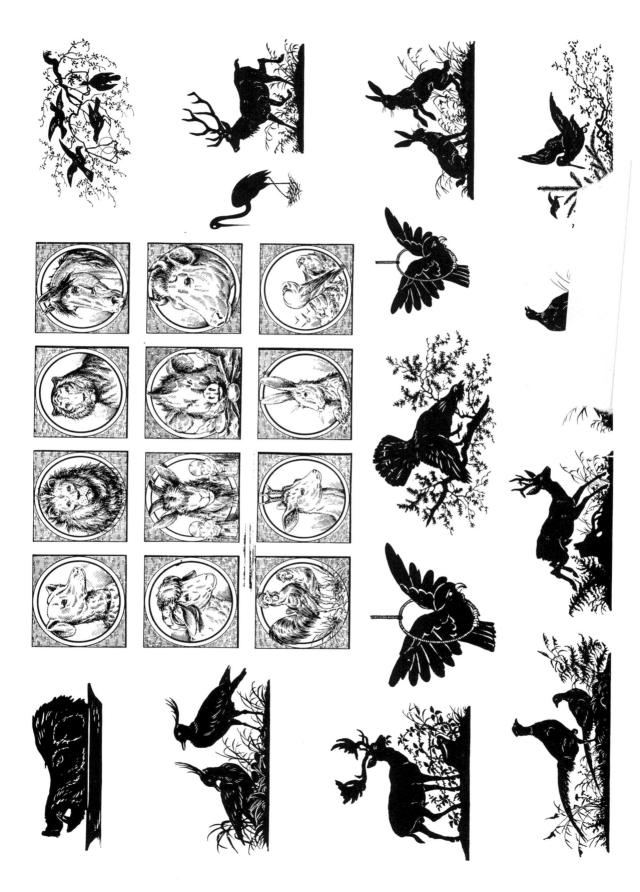

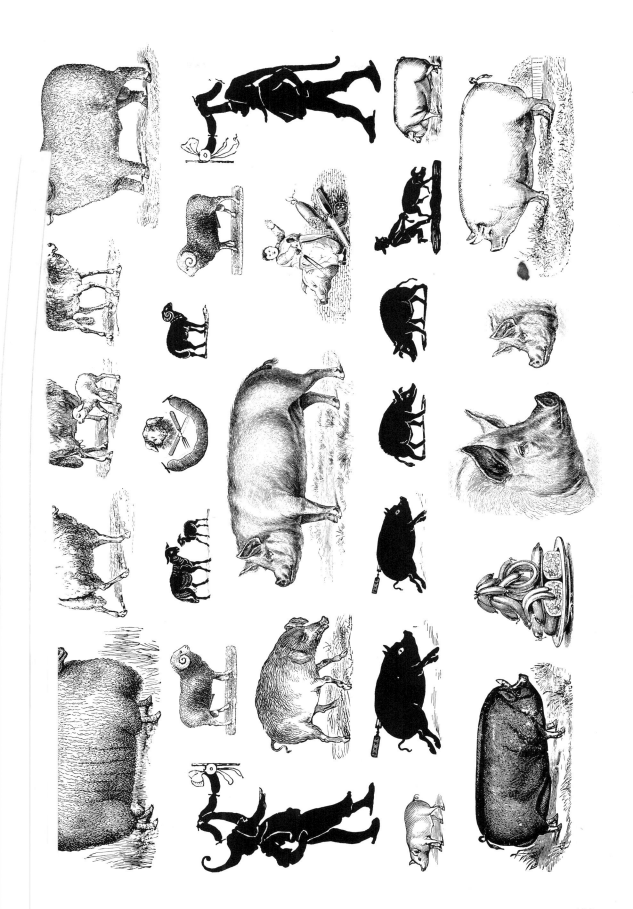

192

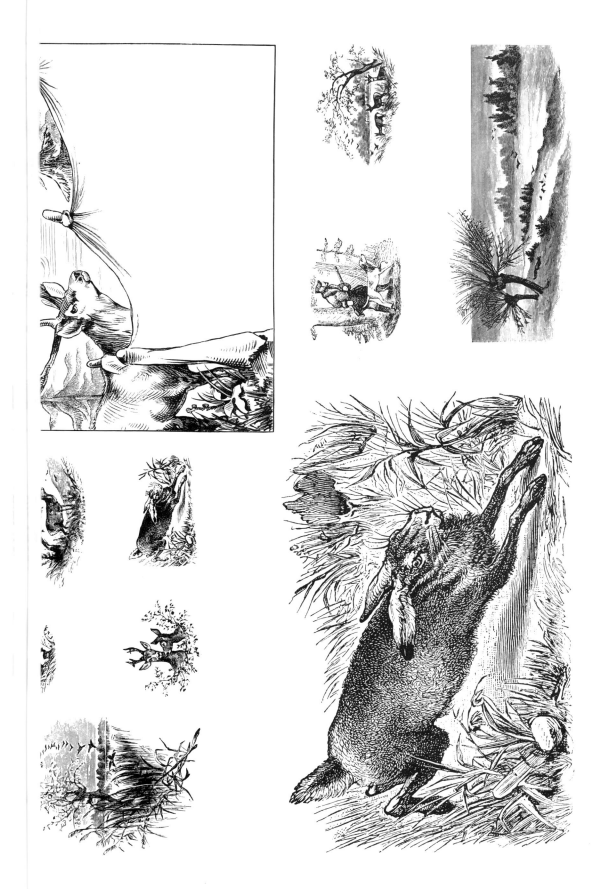

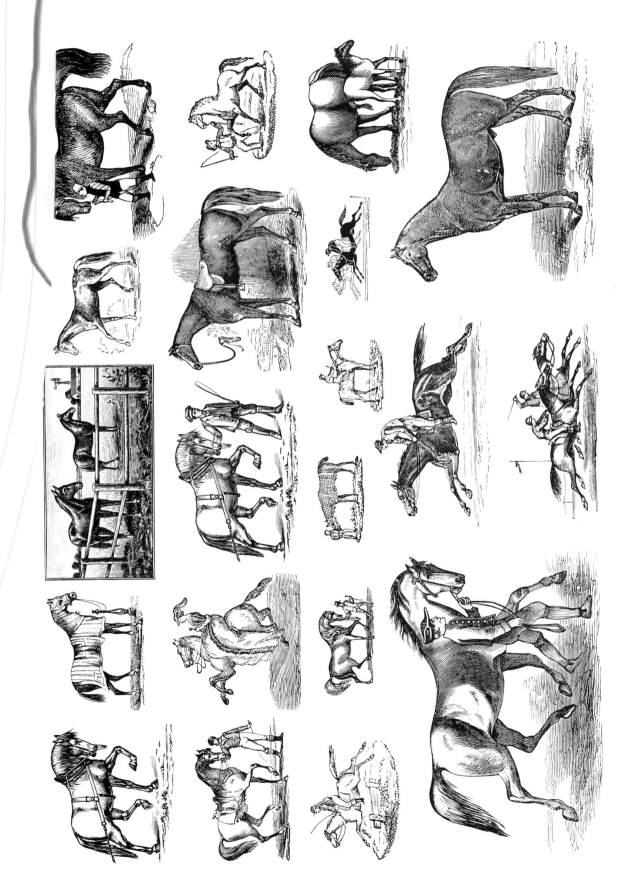

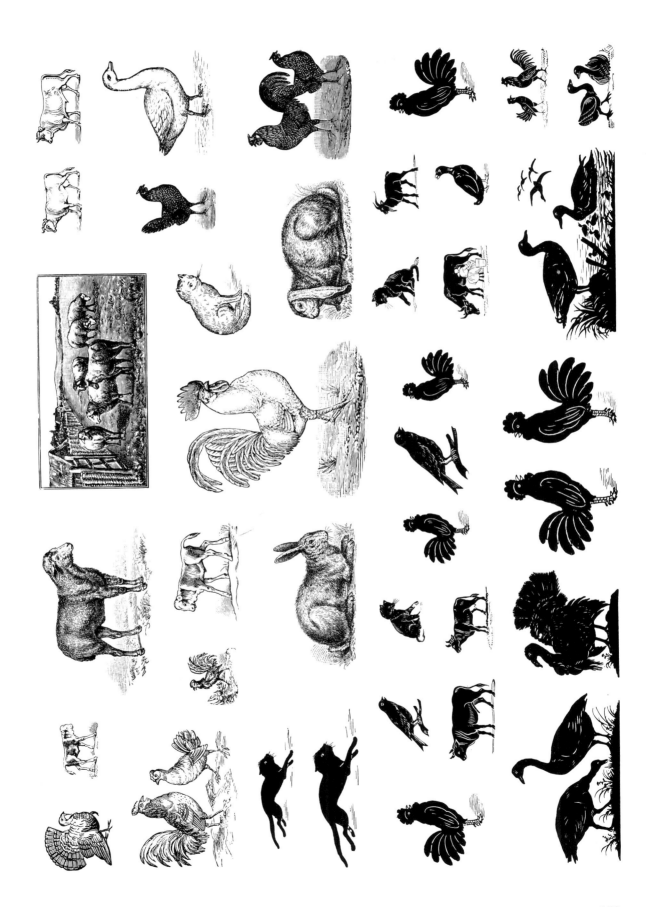

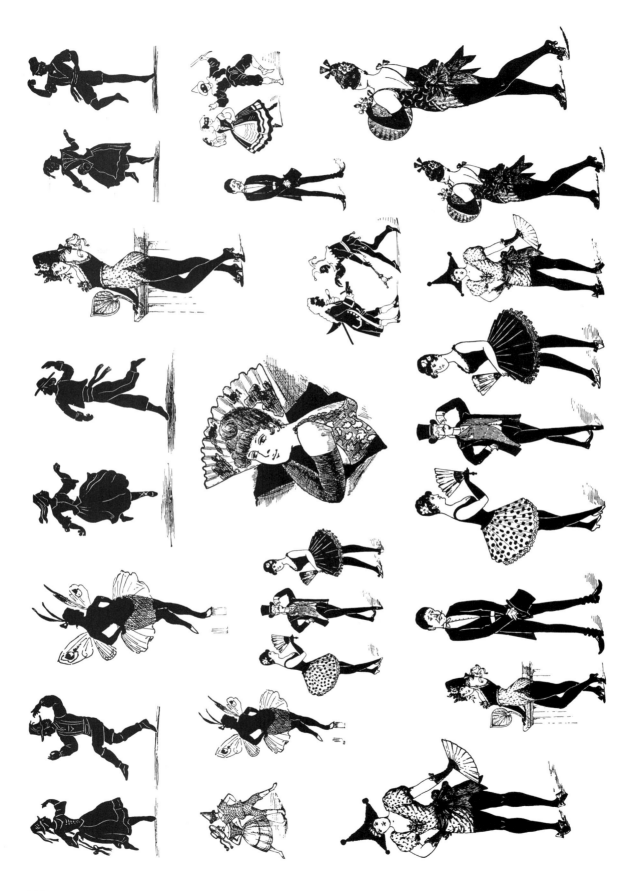

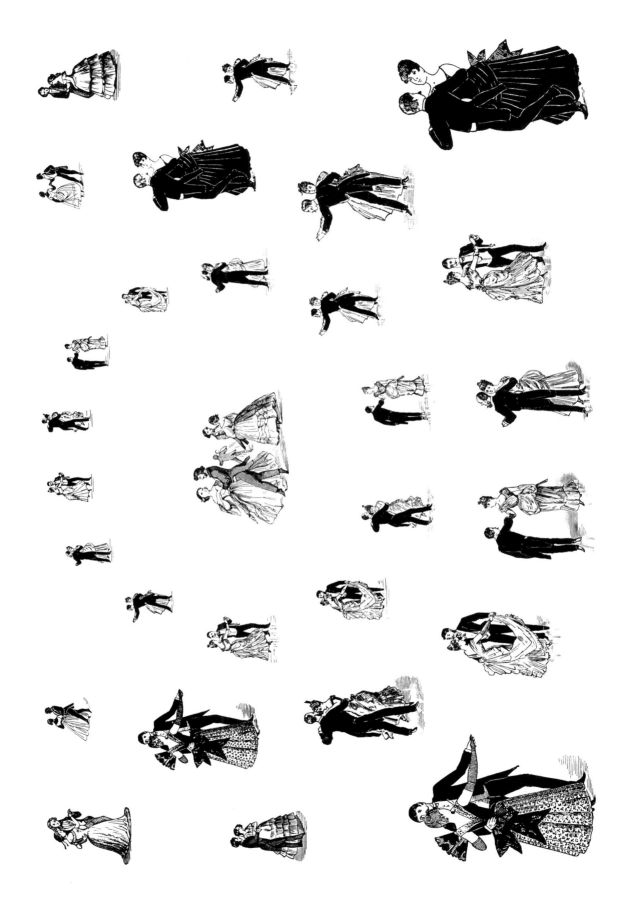

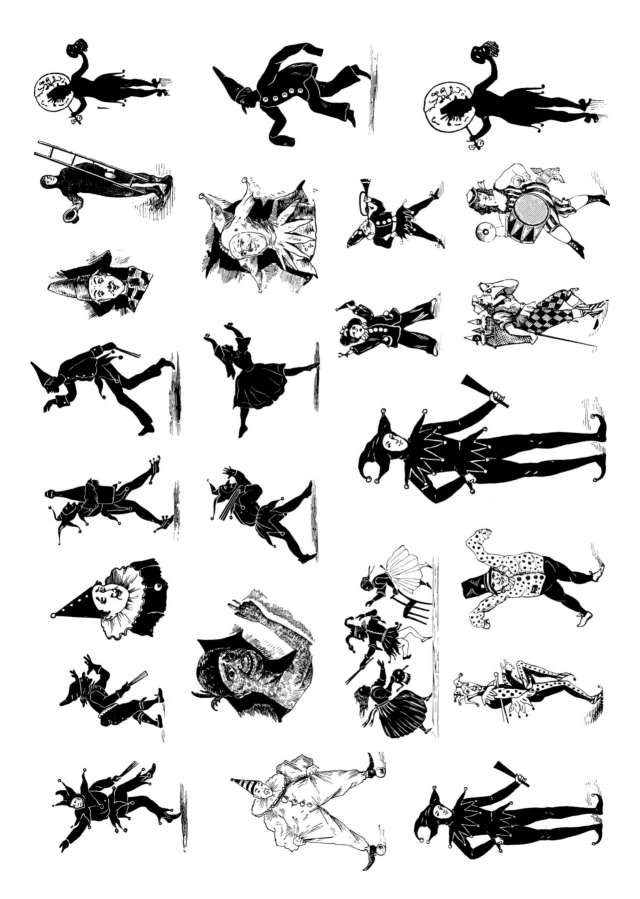

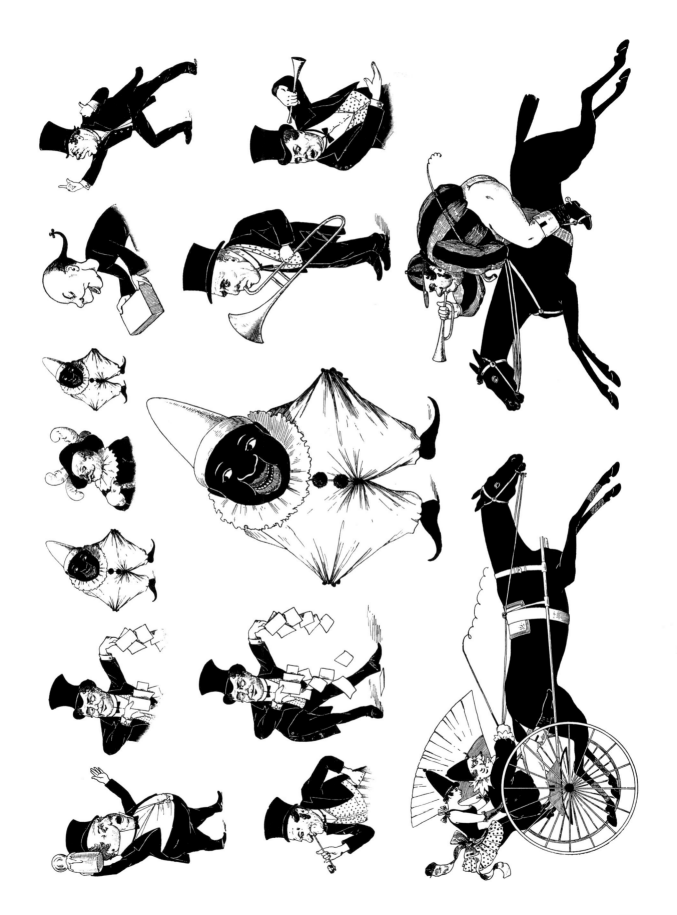

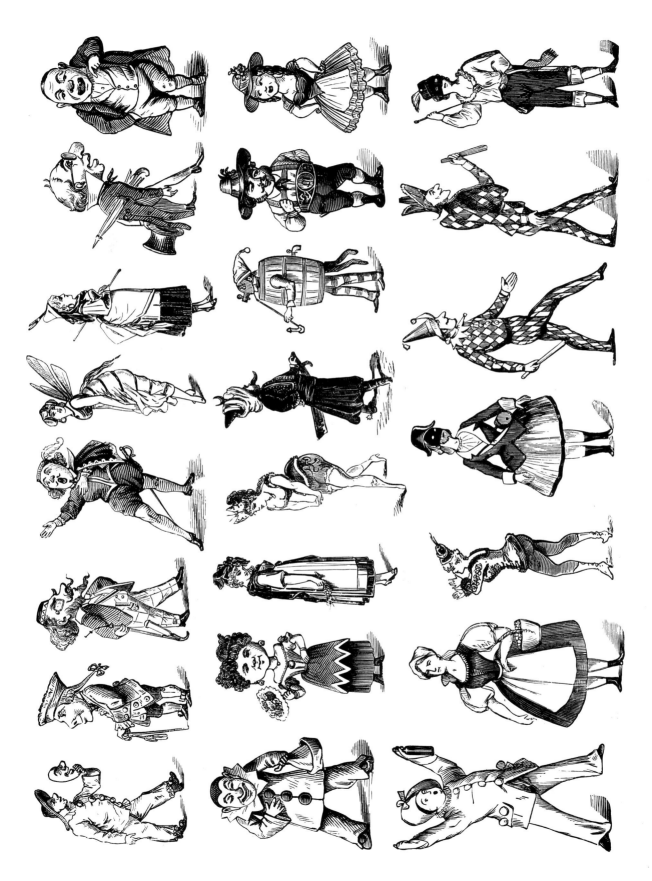

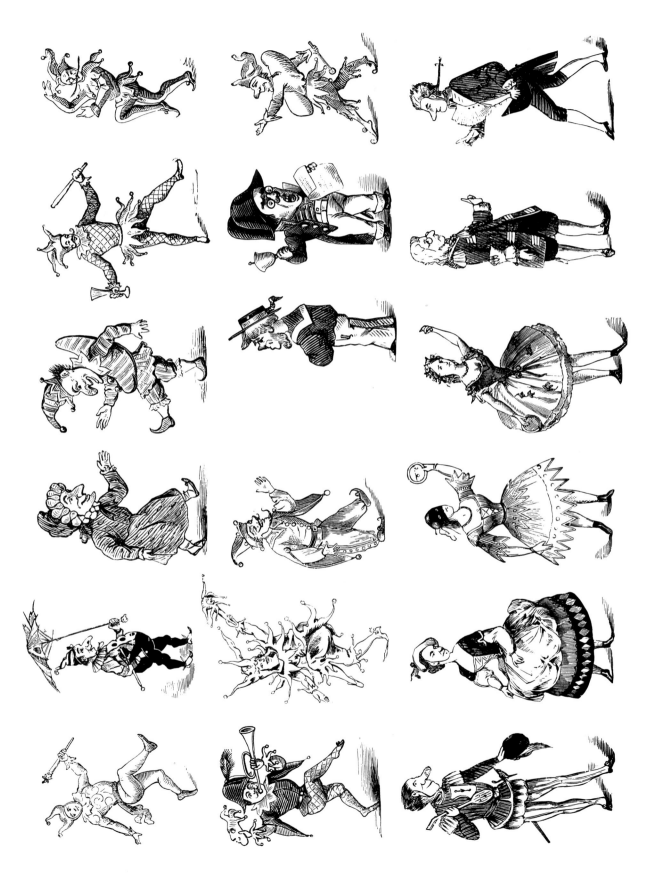

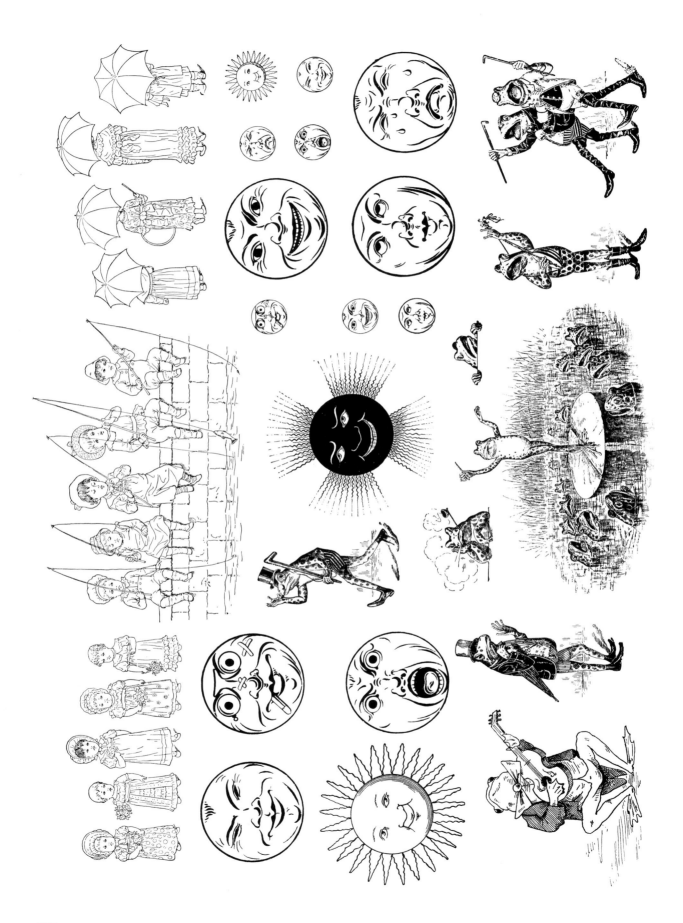

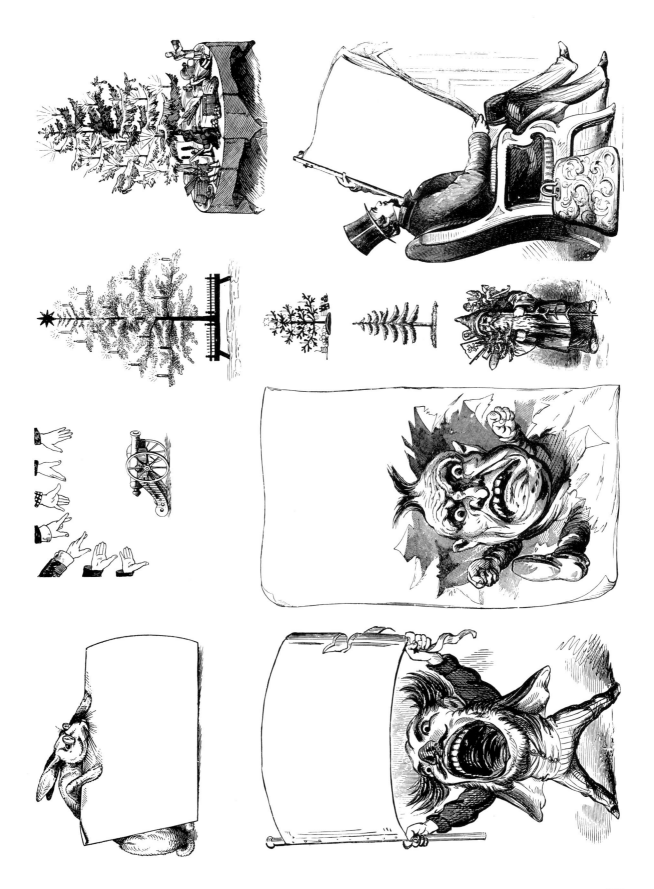

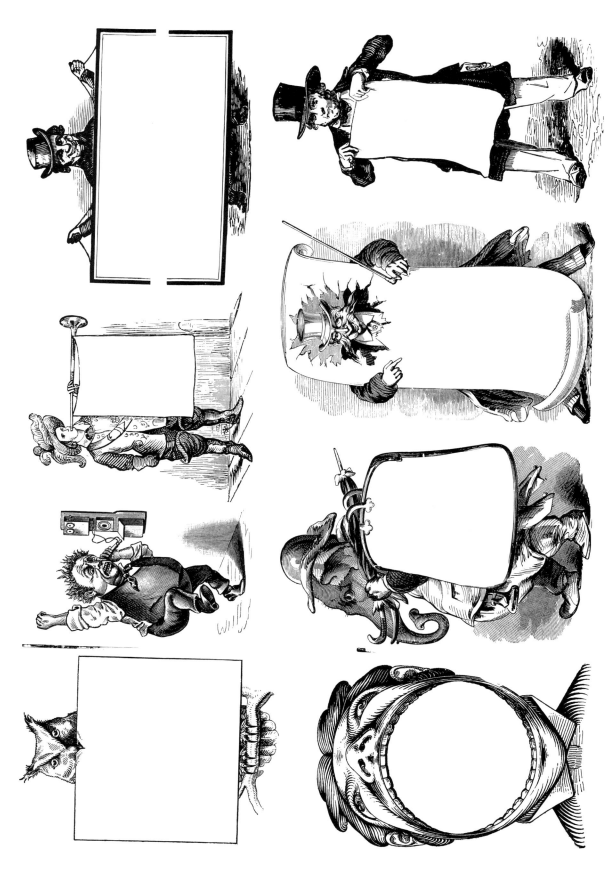

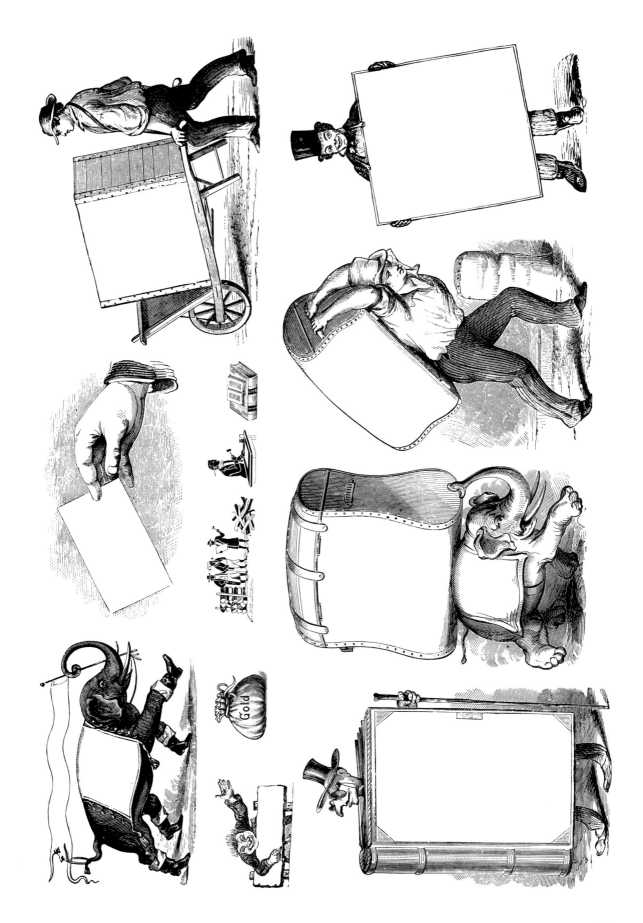

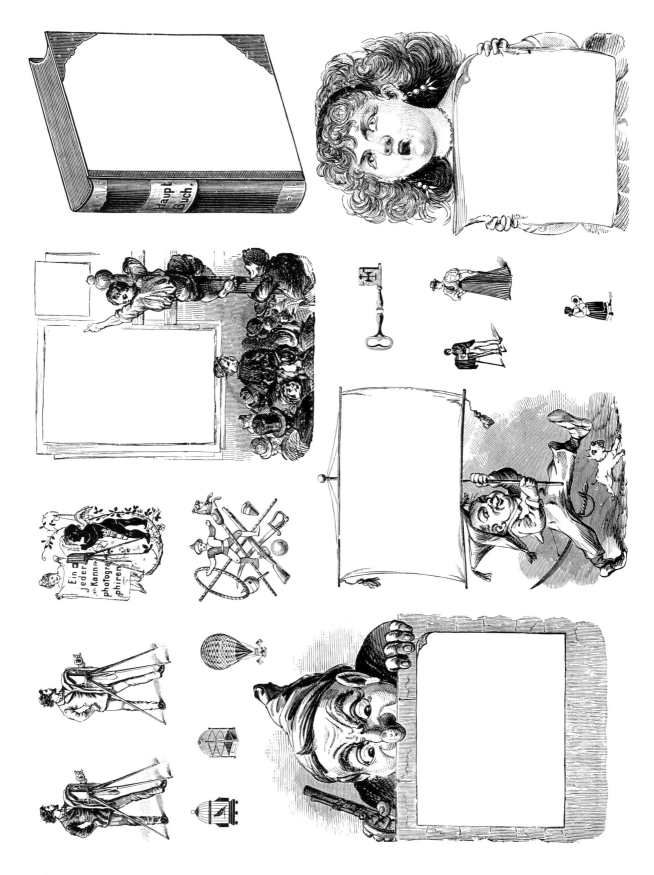

KUNST-SPEISEFETT

Glas

L. S.

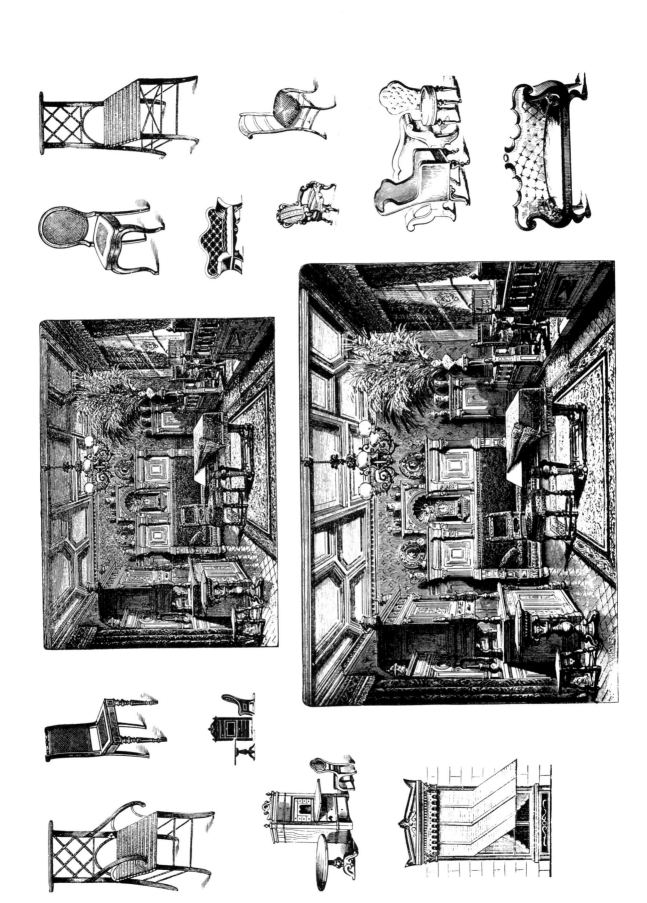

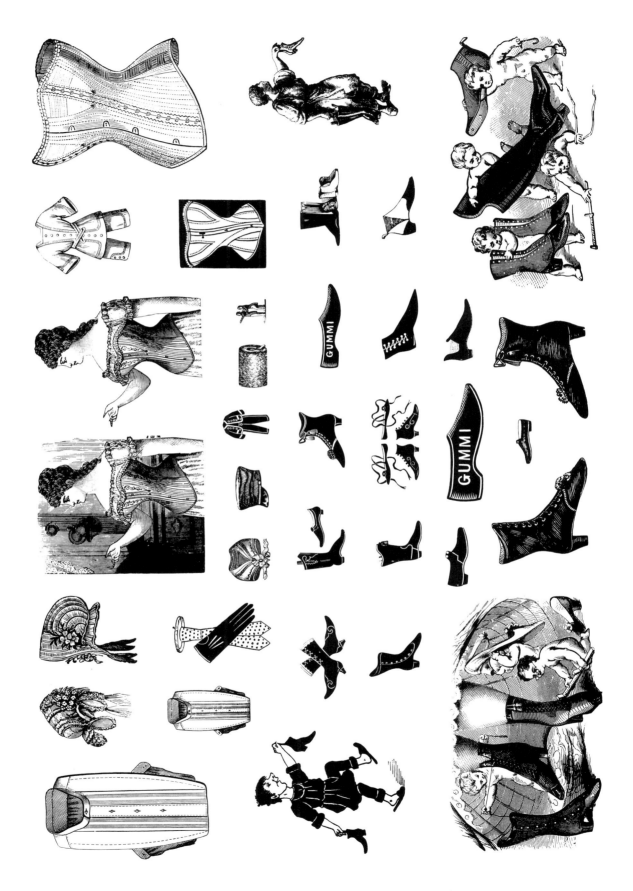

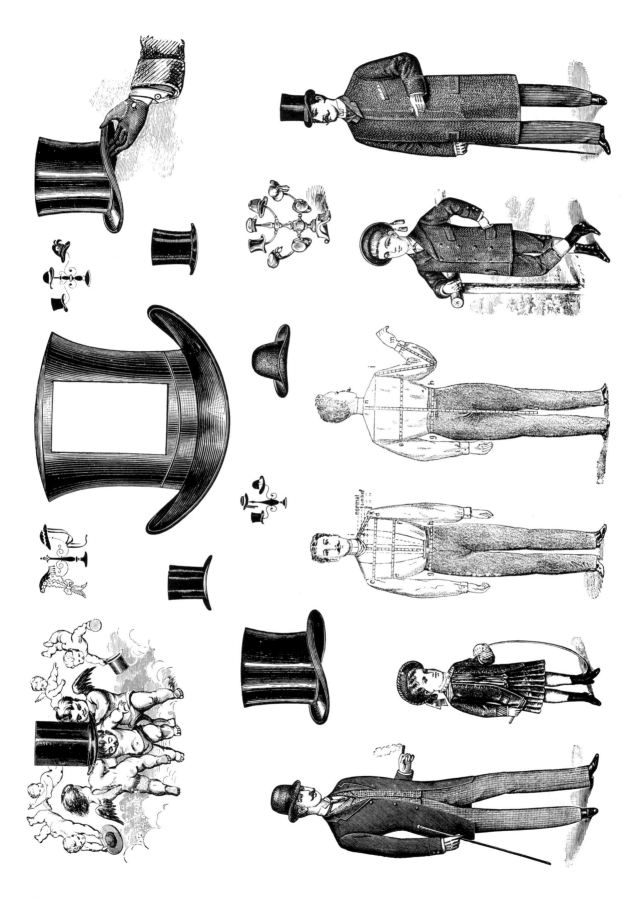

223

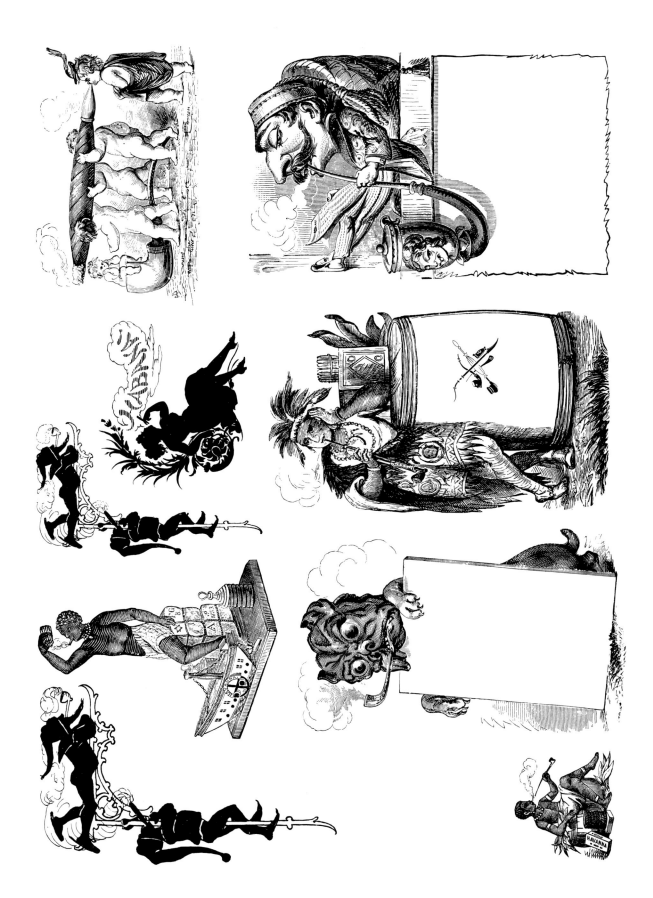

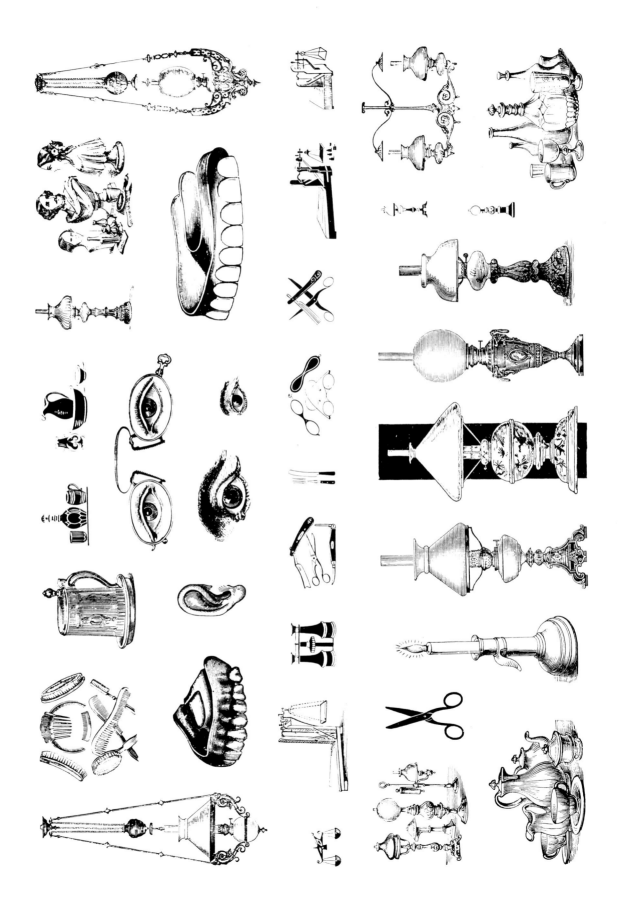

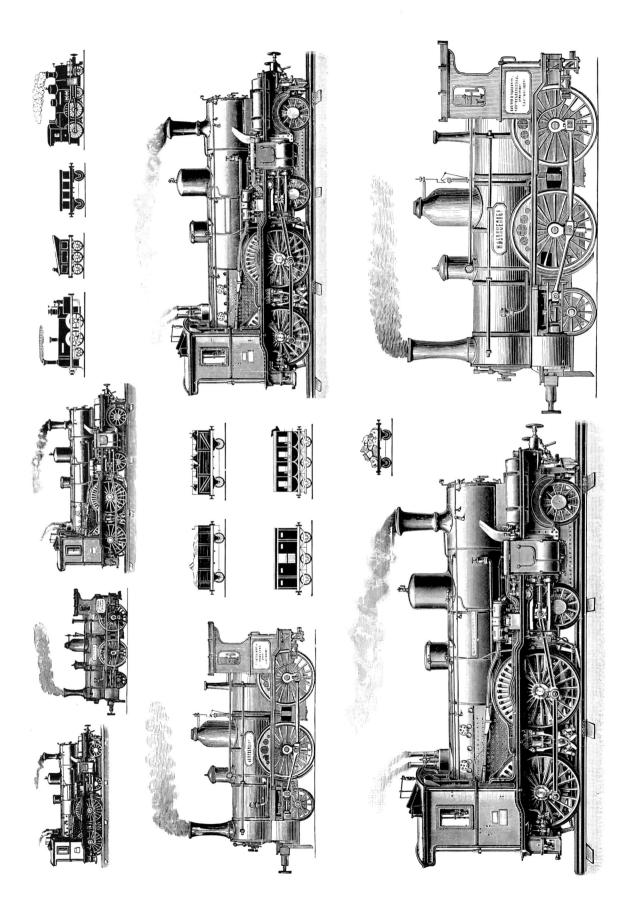

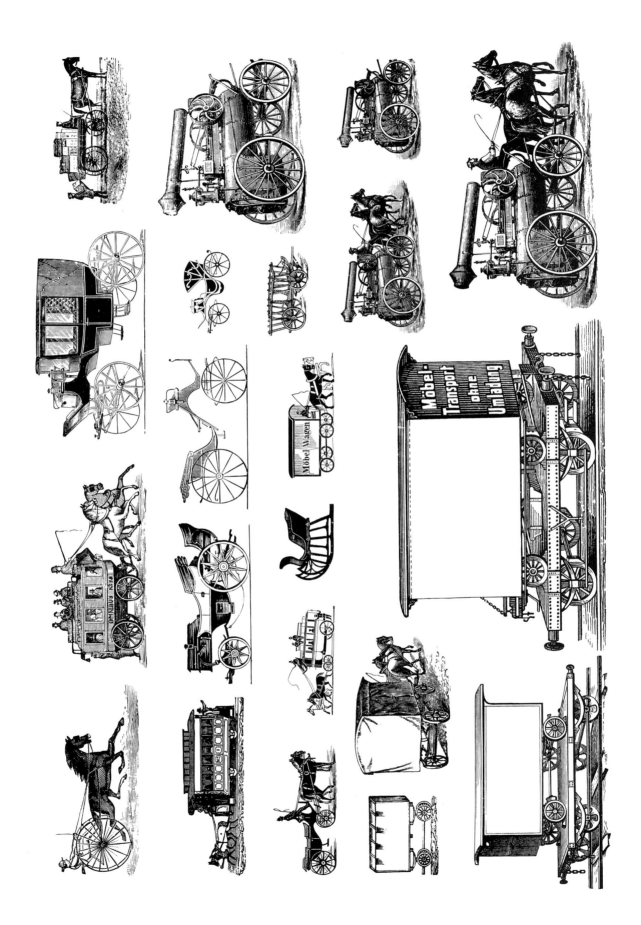

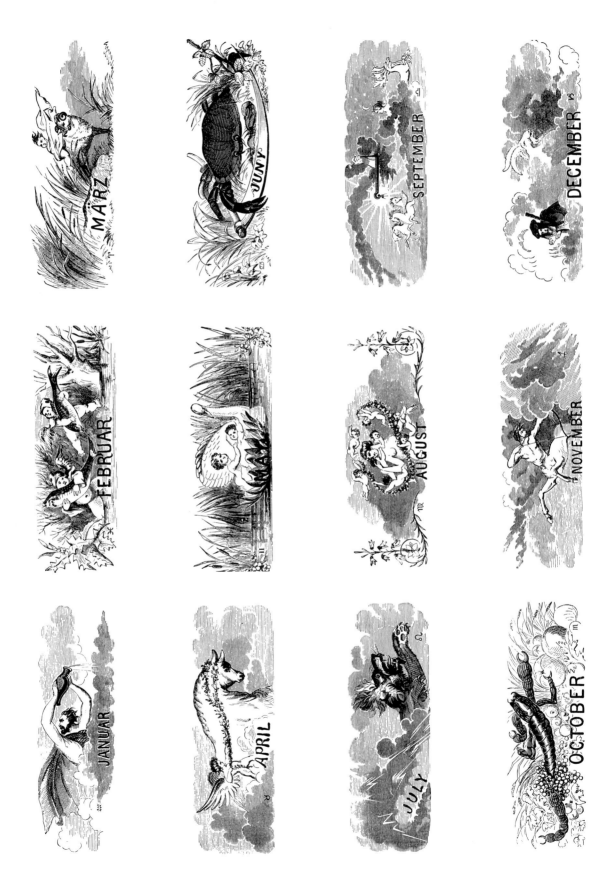

233

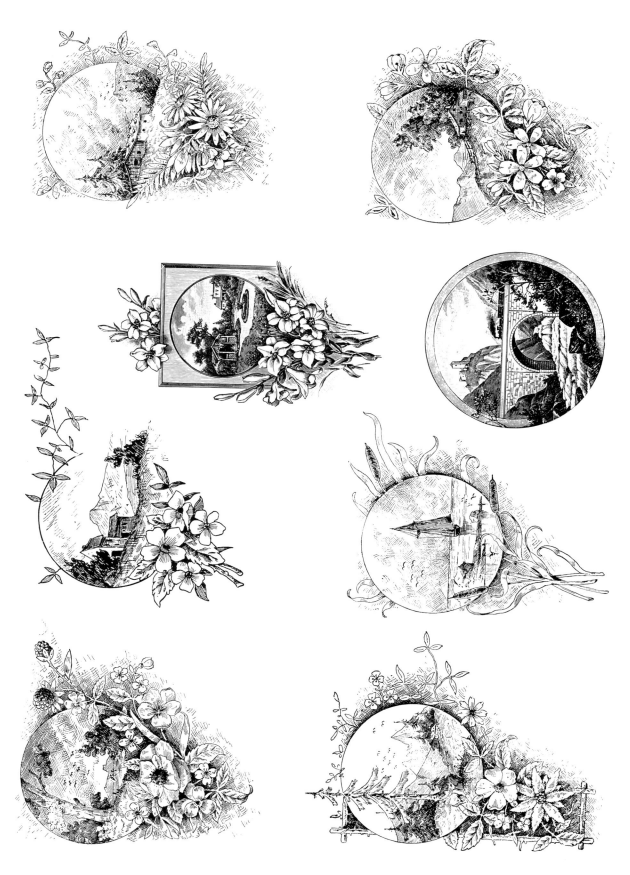

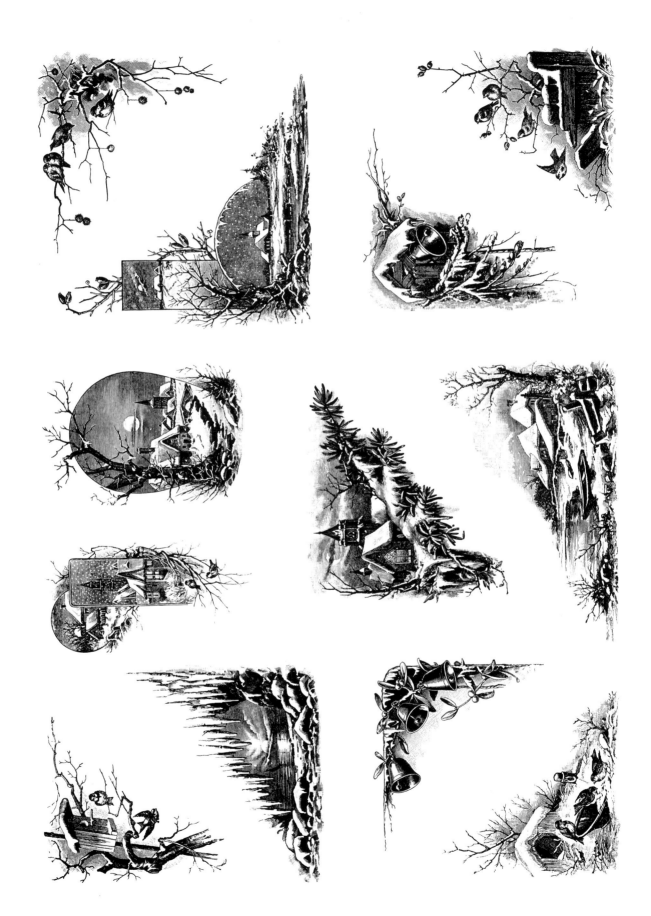

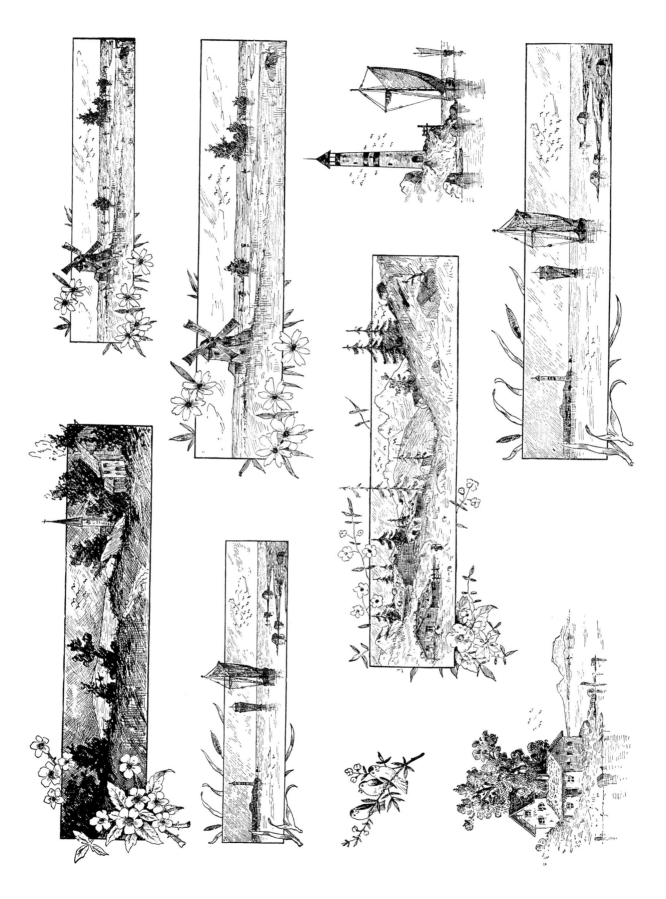

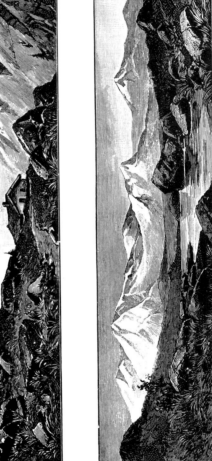

248

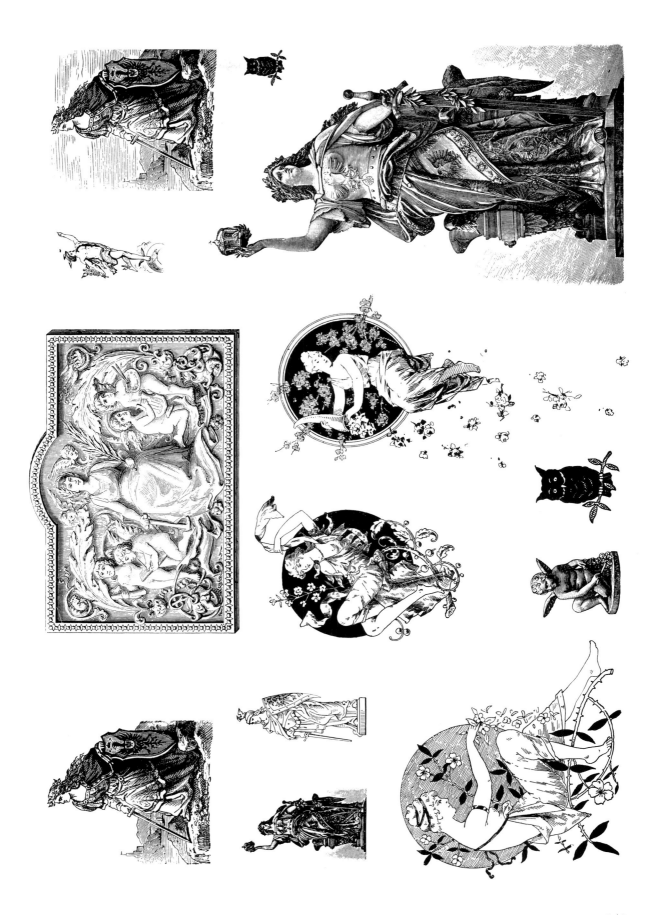

252

1/2 + 1/2 SIZE.

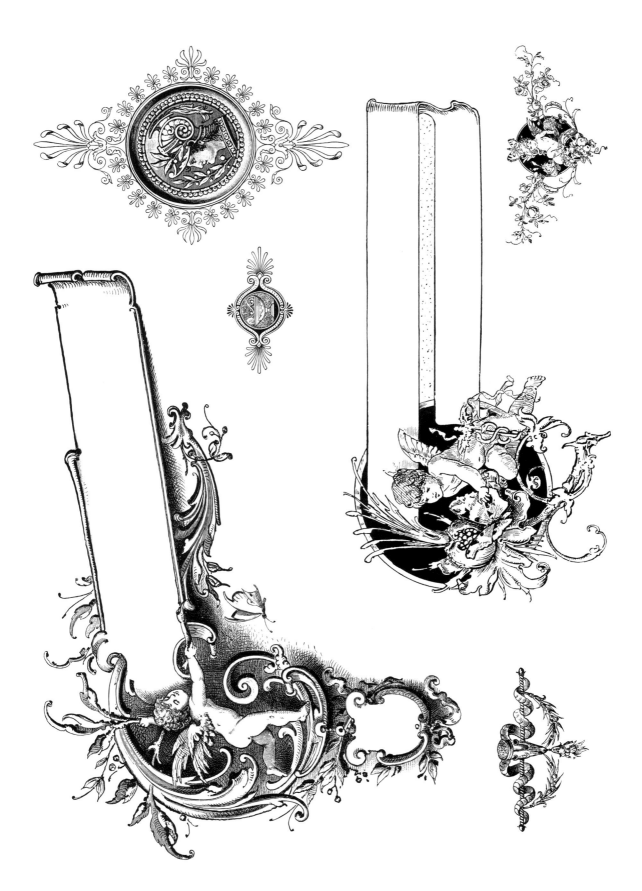

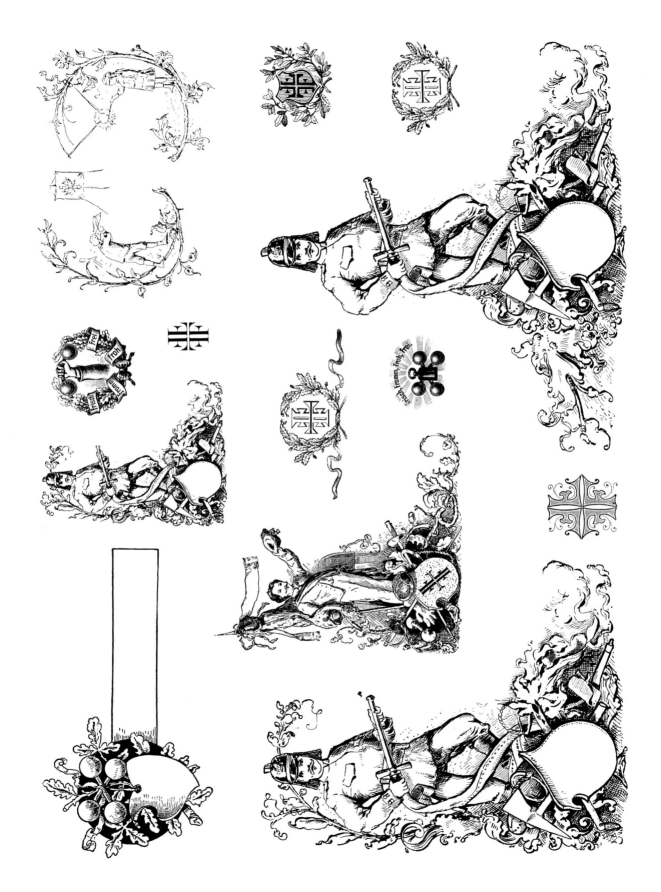

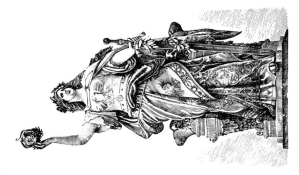

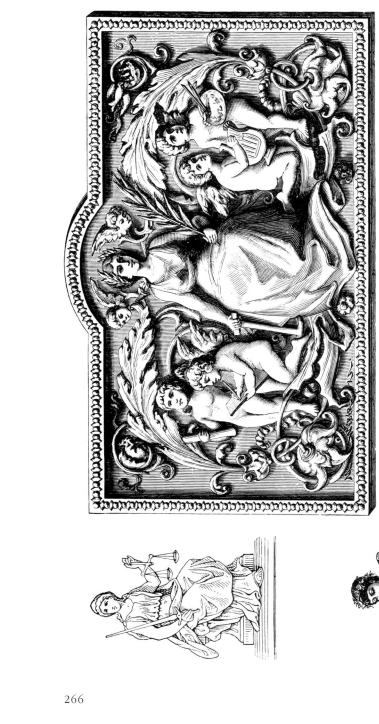

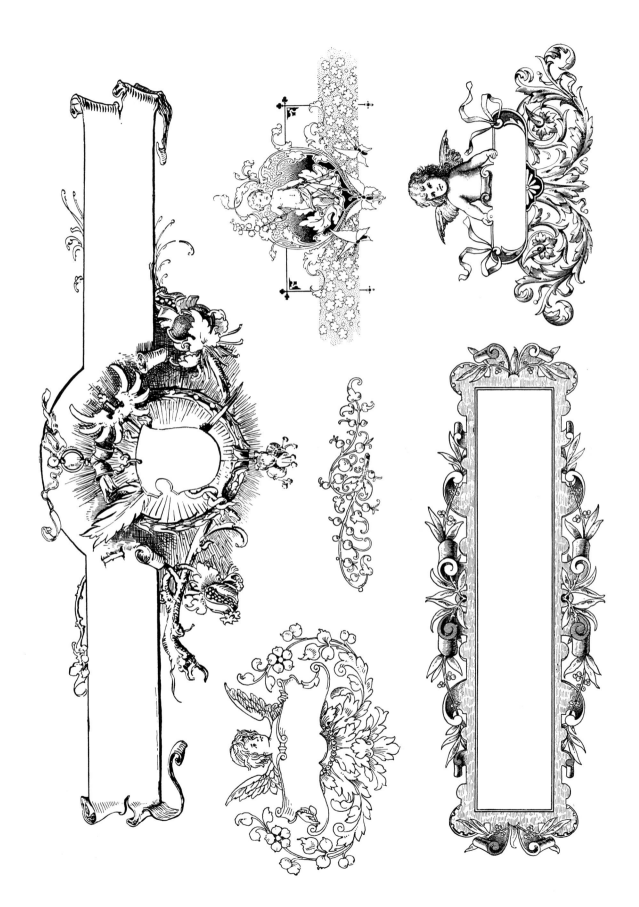

Theophil Noster

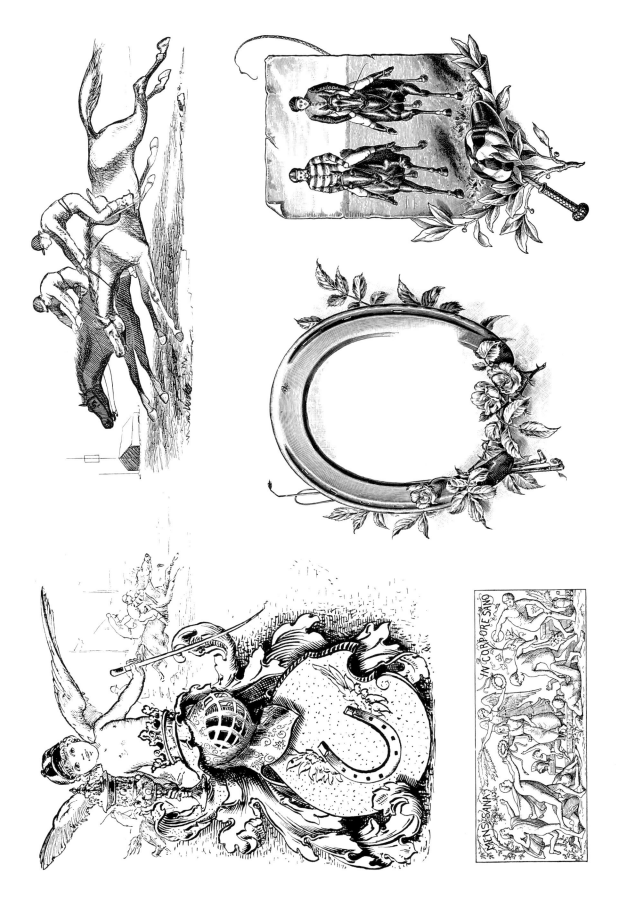

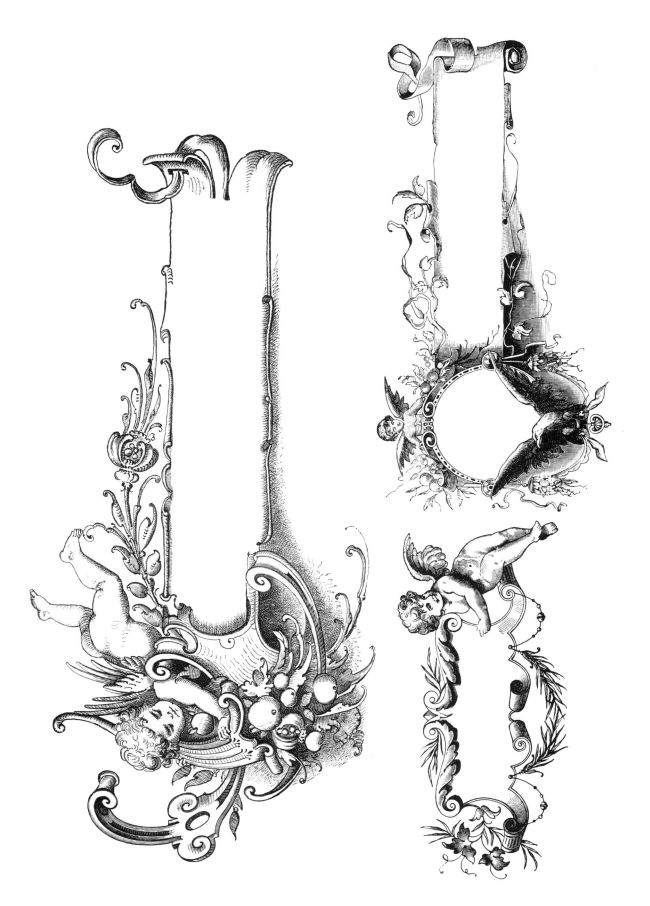

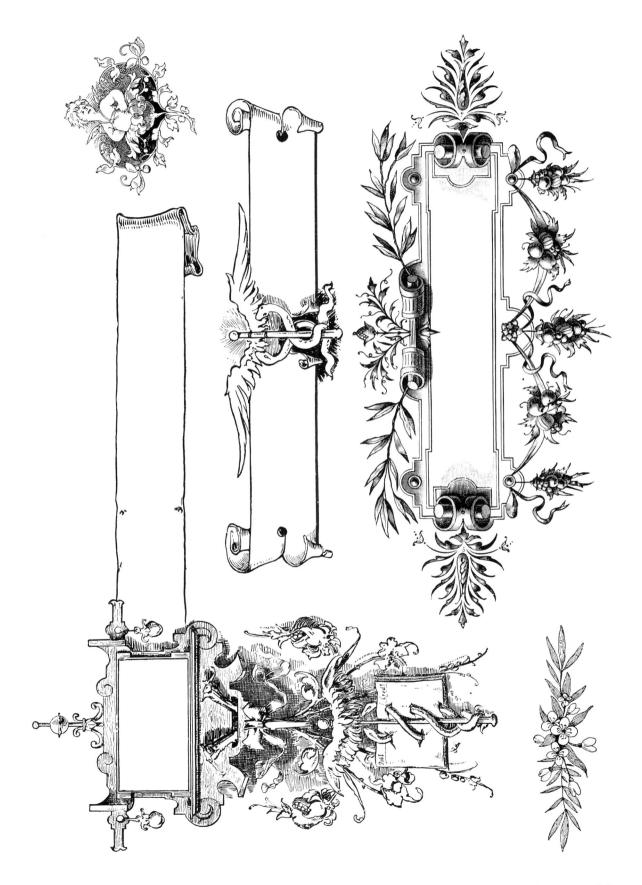

276

279

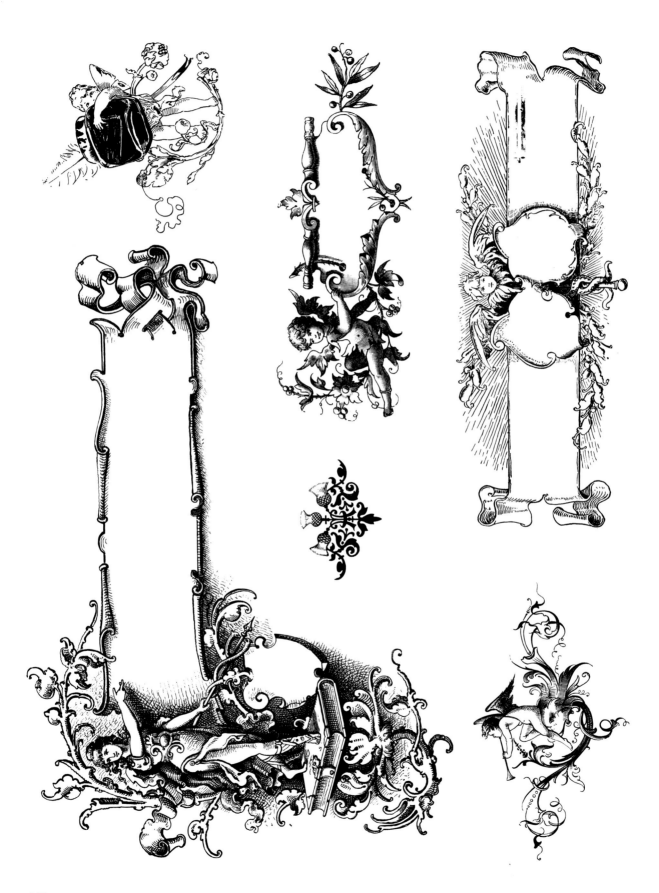

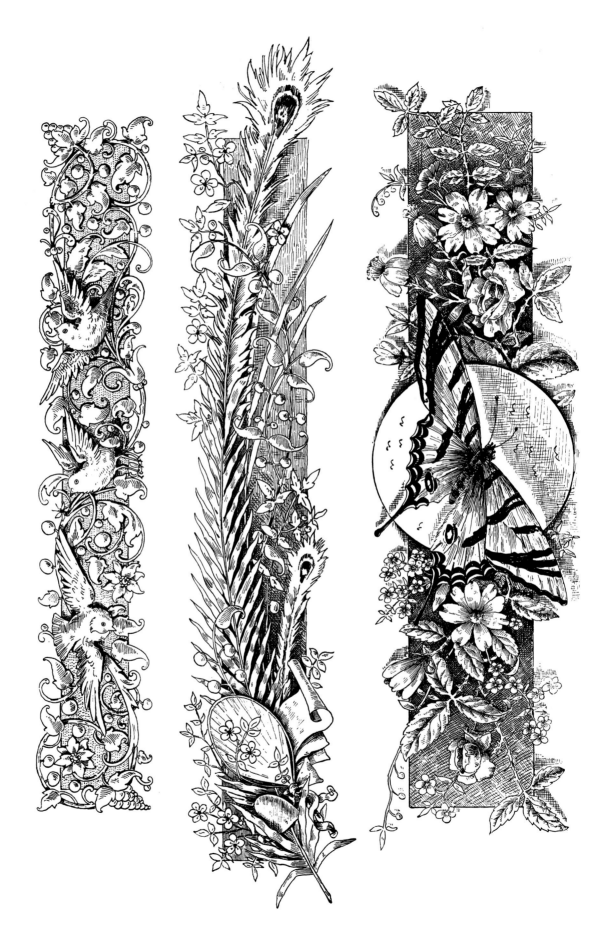

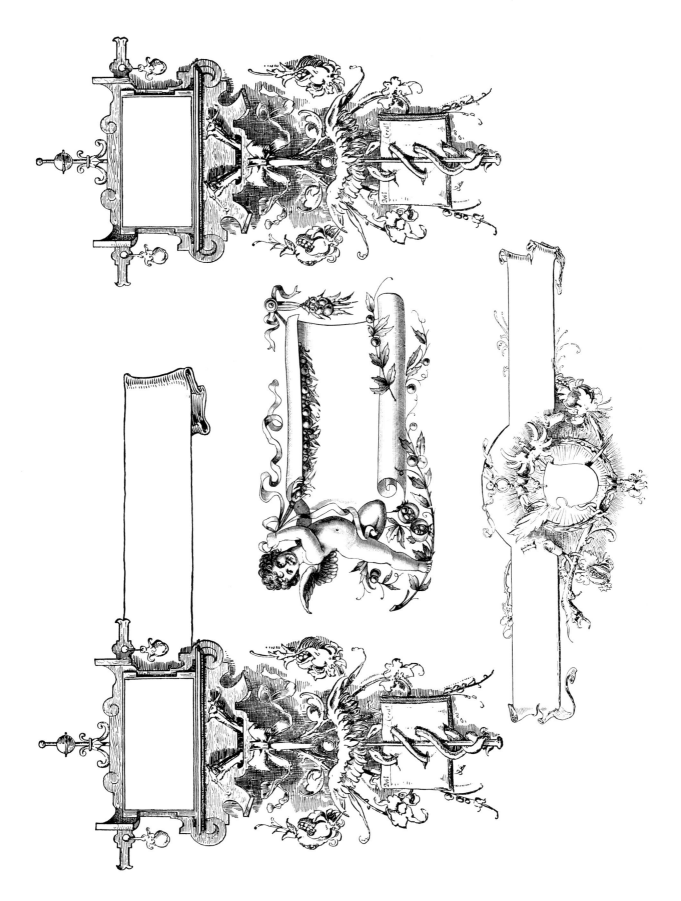

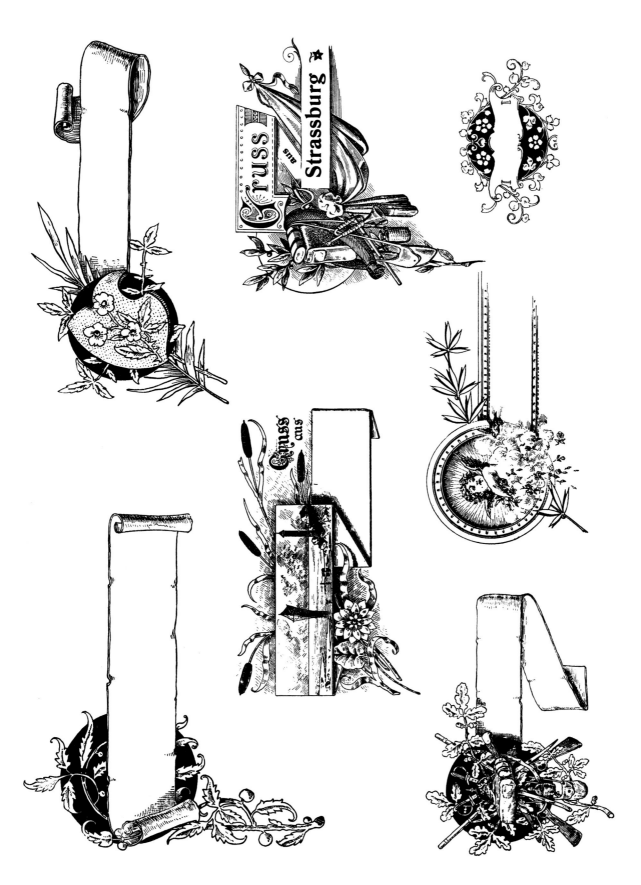

Gruss aus Strassburg

Gruss aus

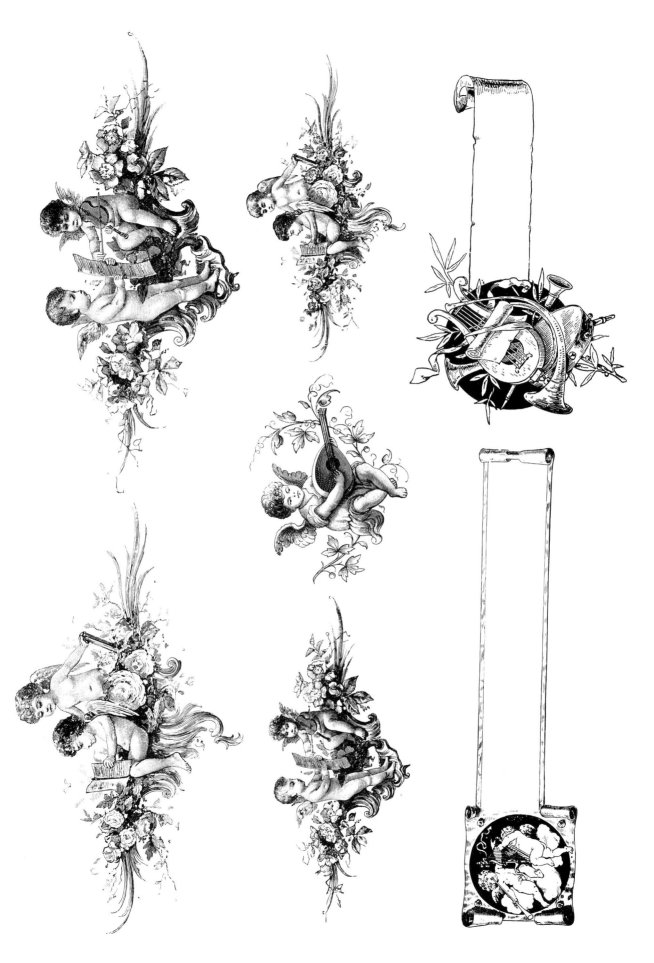

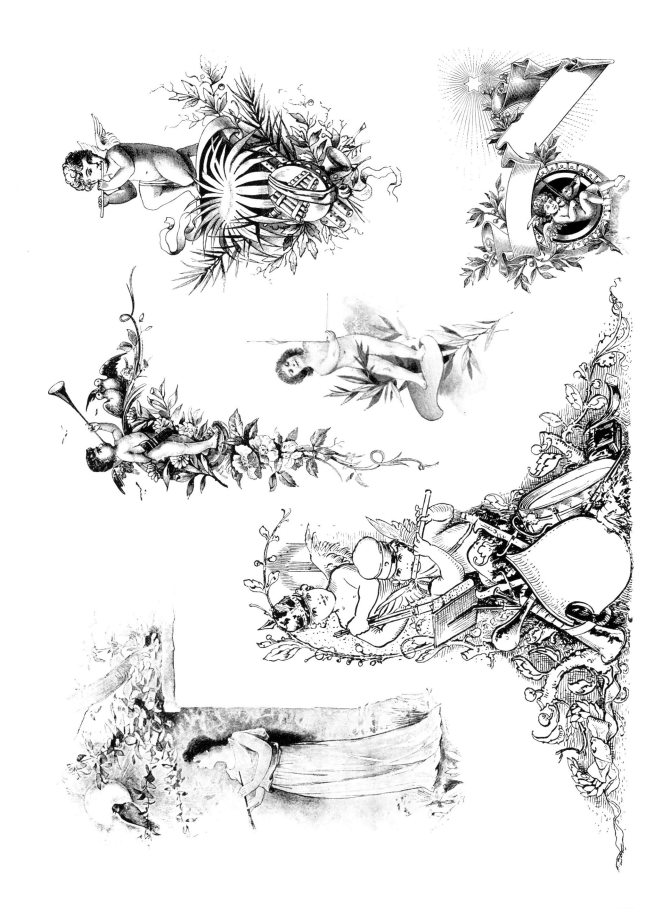

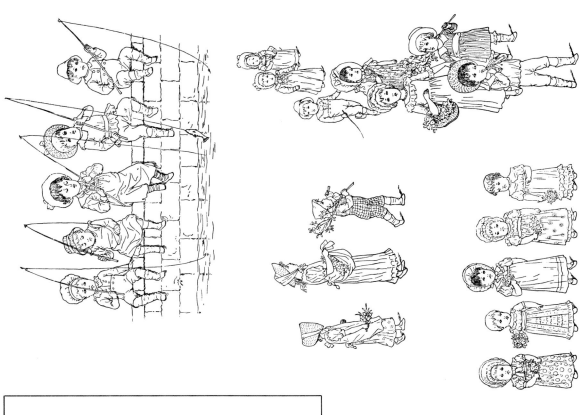

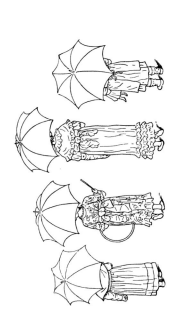

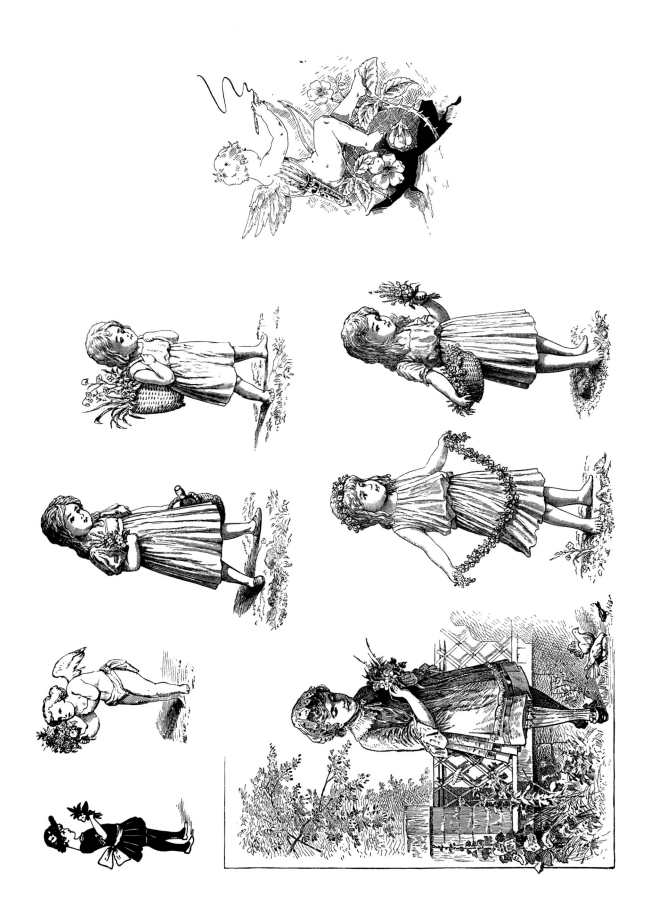

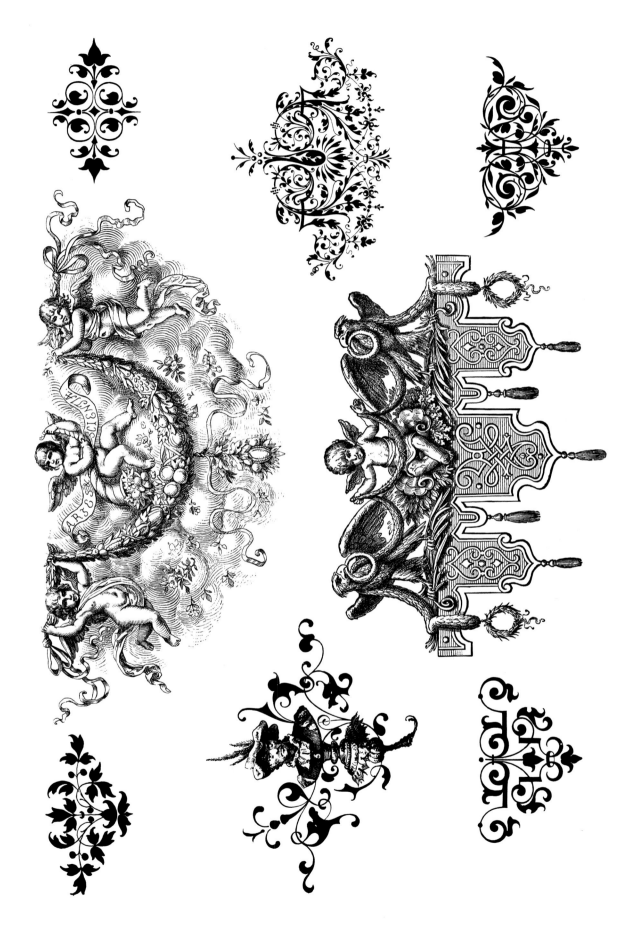

298

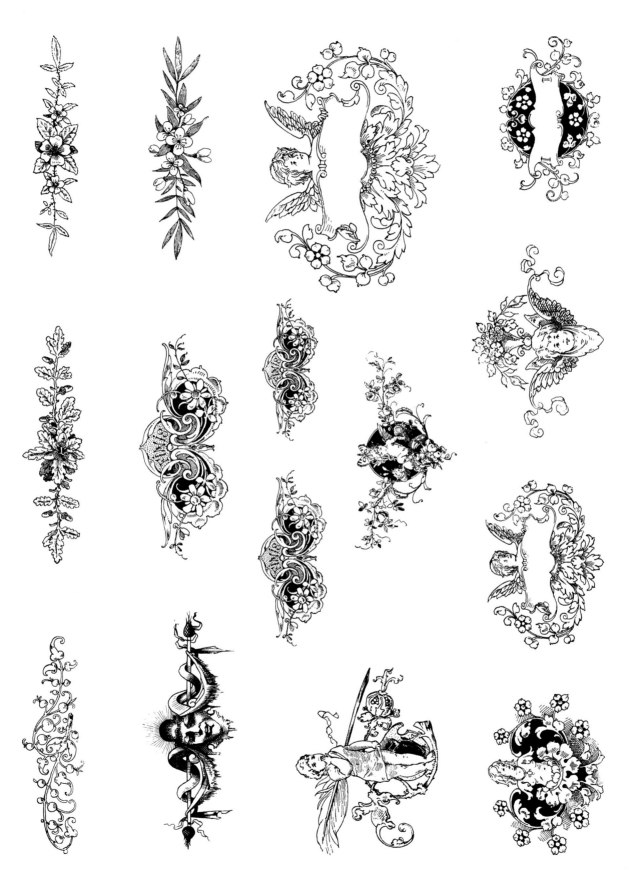

302

304

PRECIOUS PEARLS

Fare well!

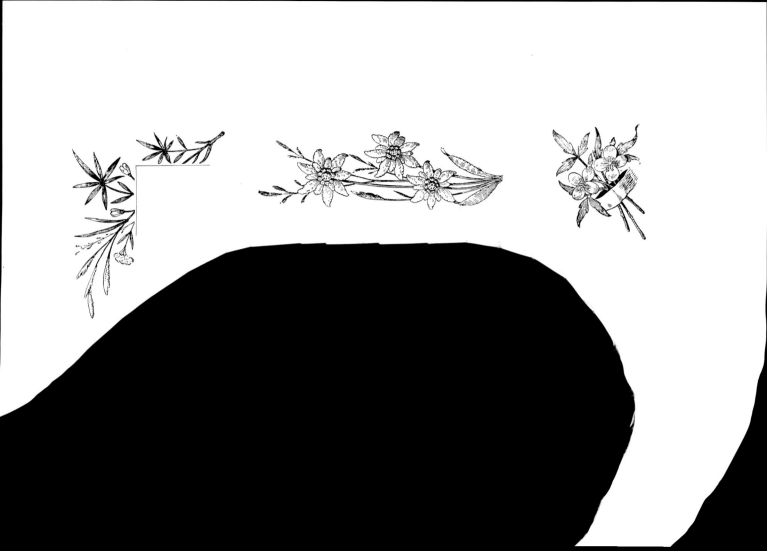

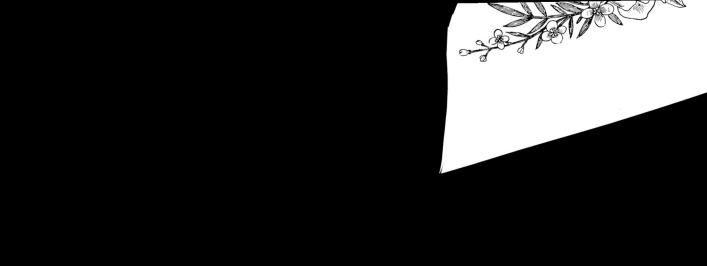

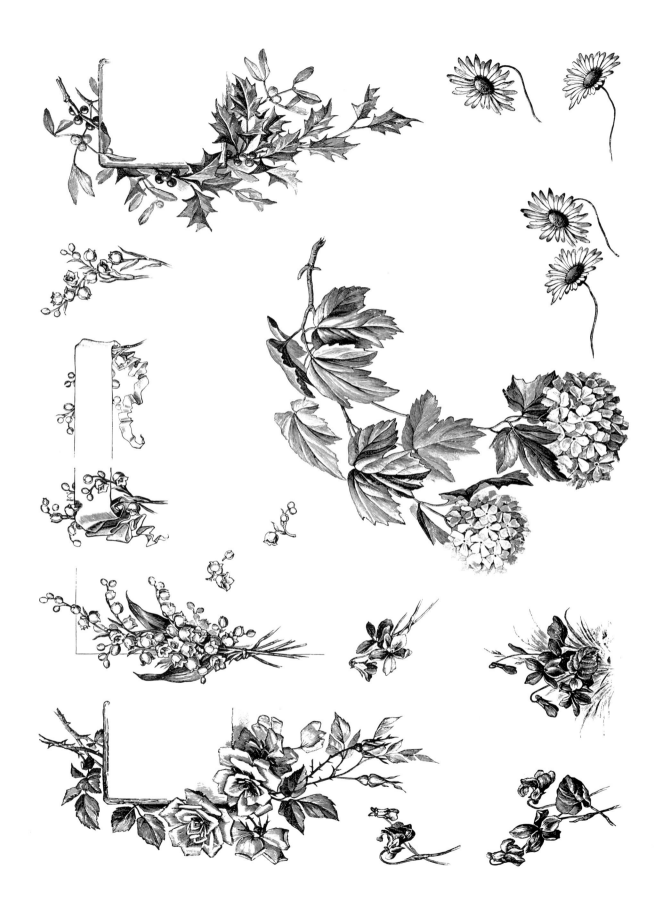

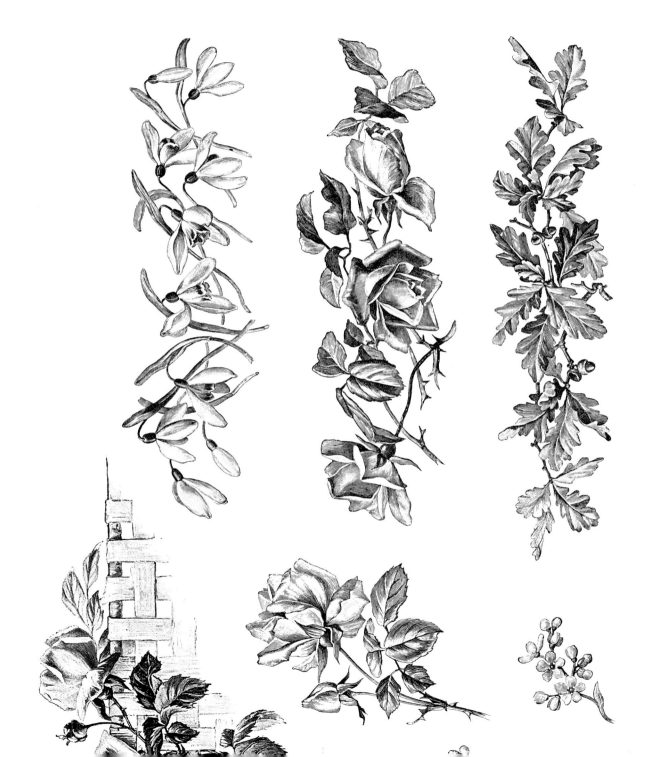

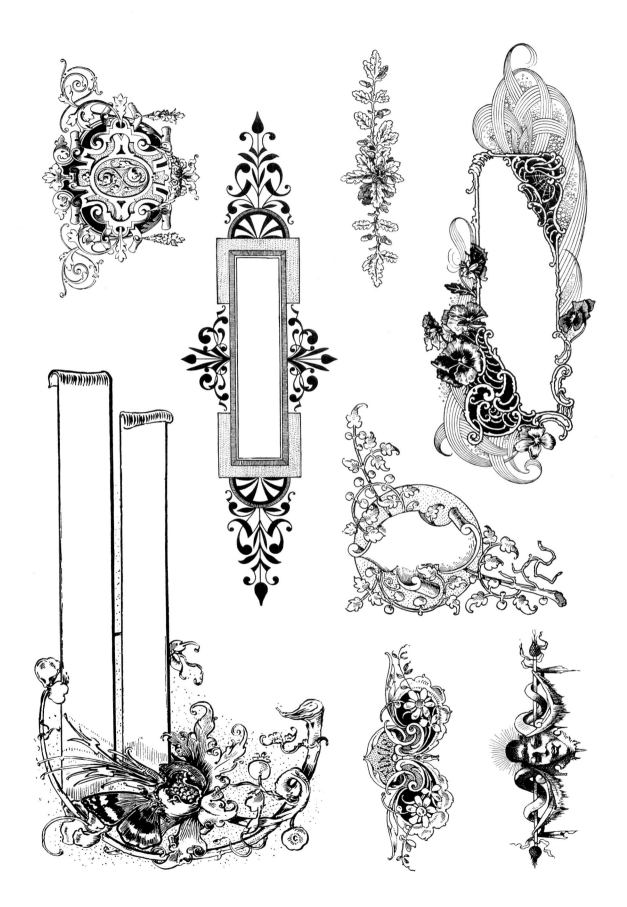

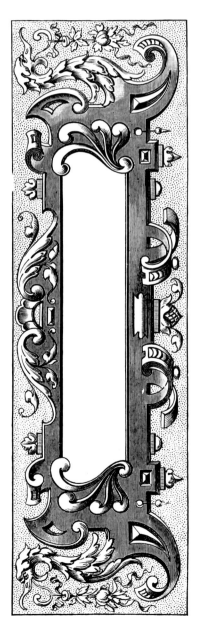

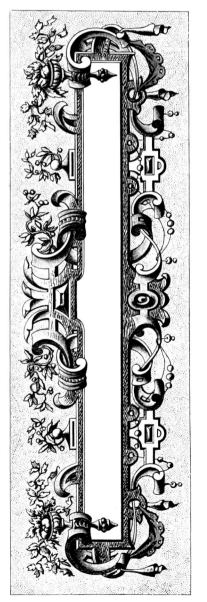

318

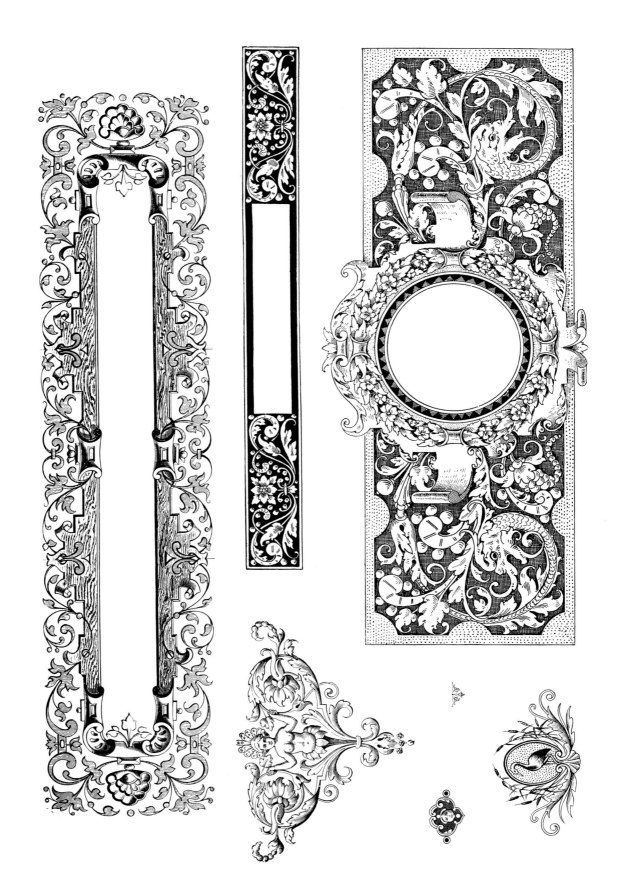

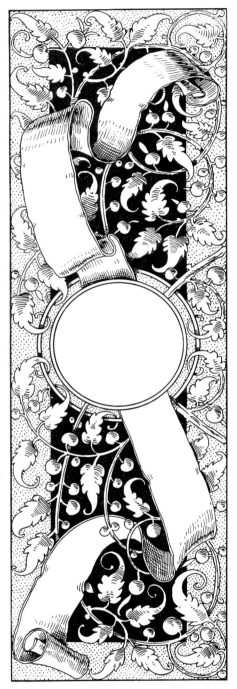

SUMMER

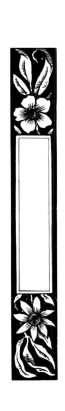

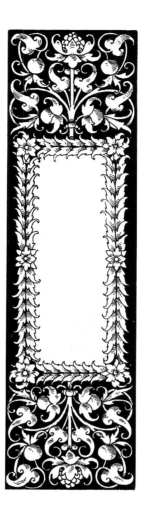

327

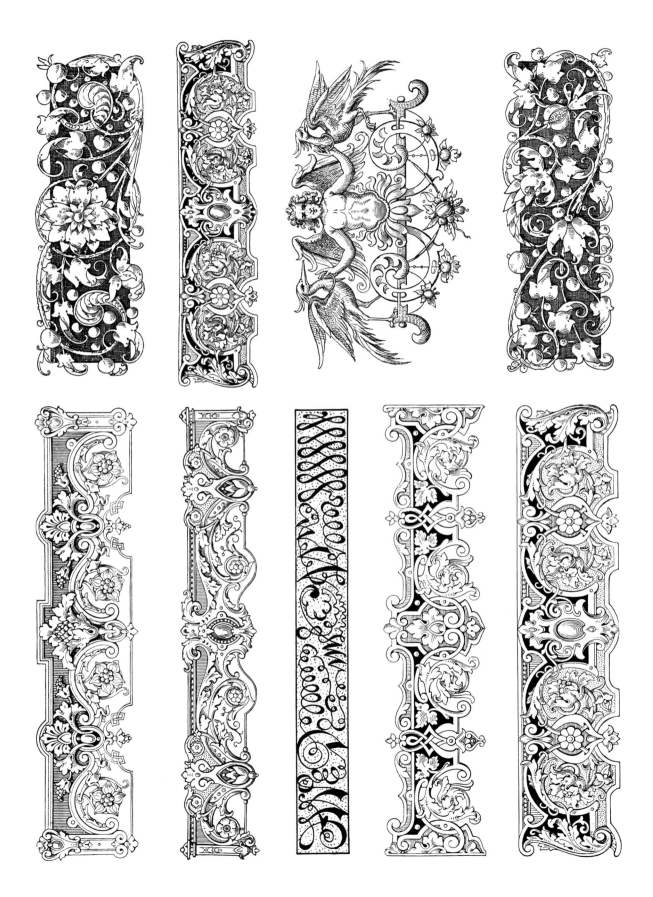

338

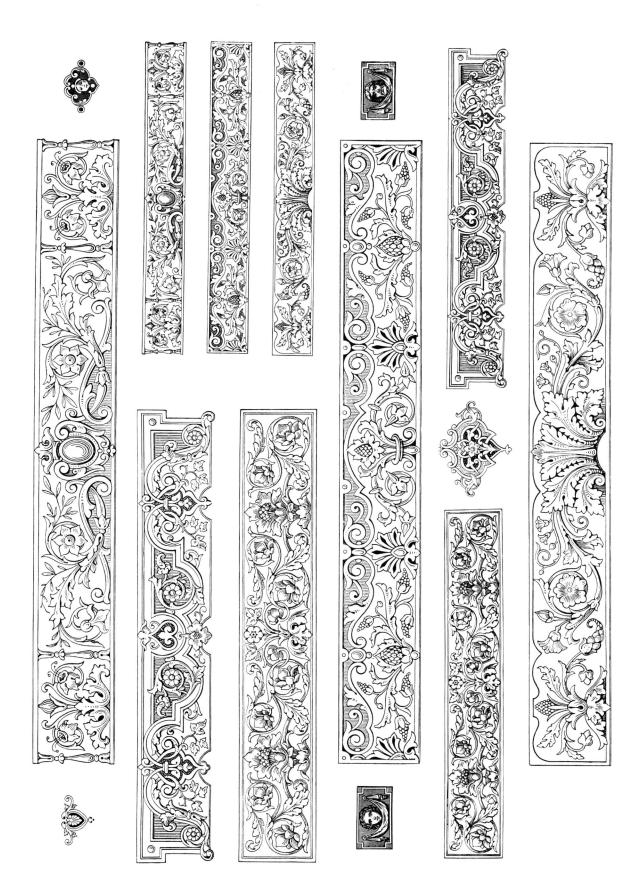

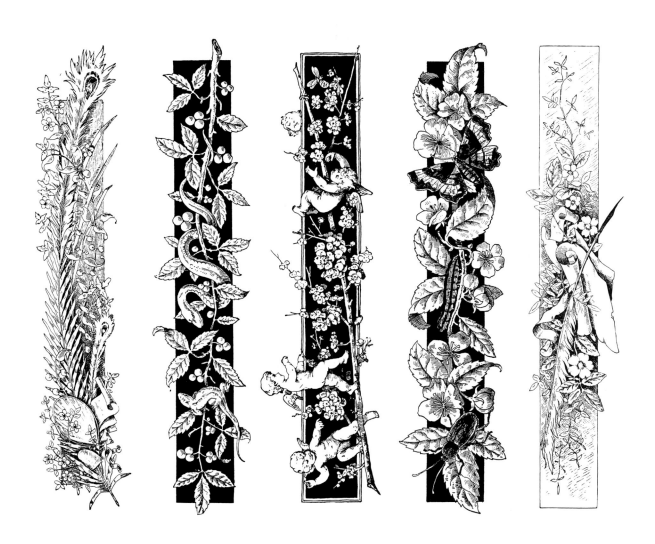

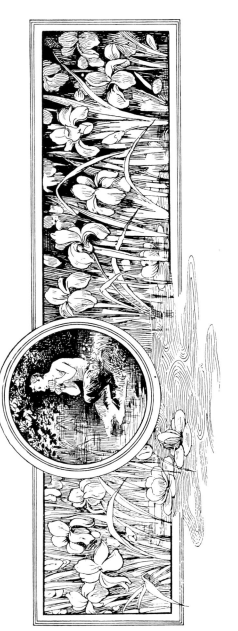

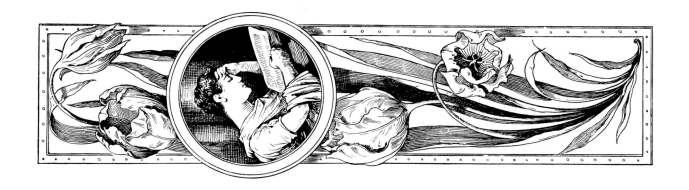

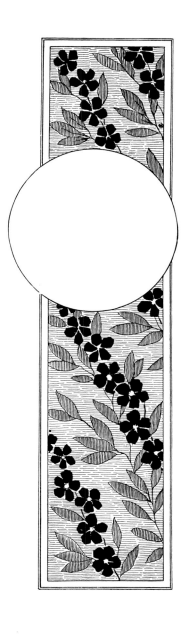

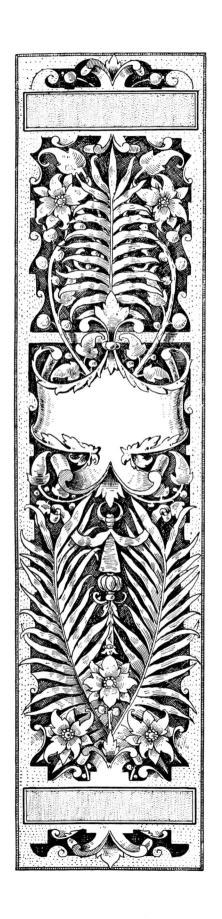

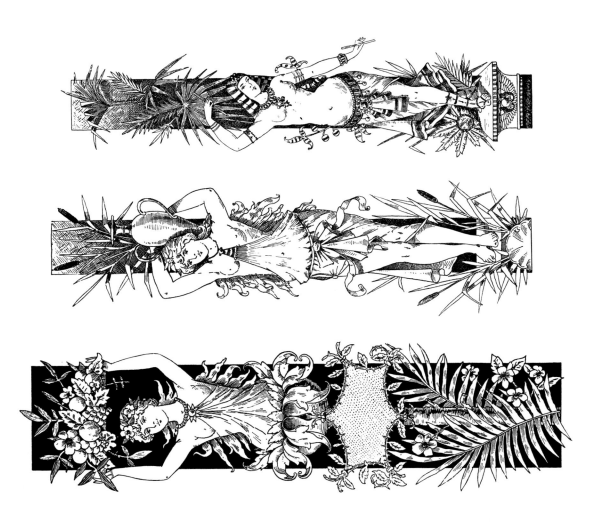

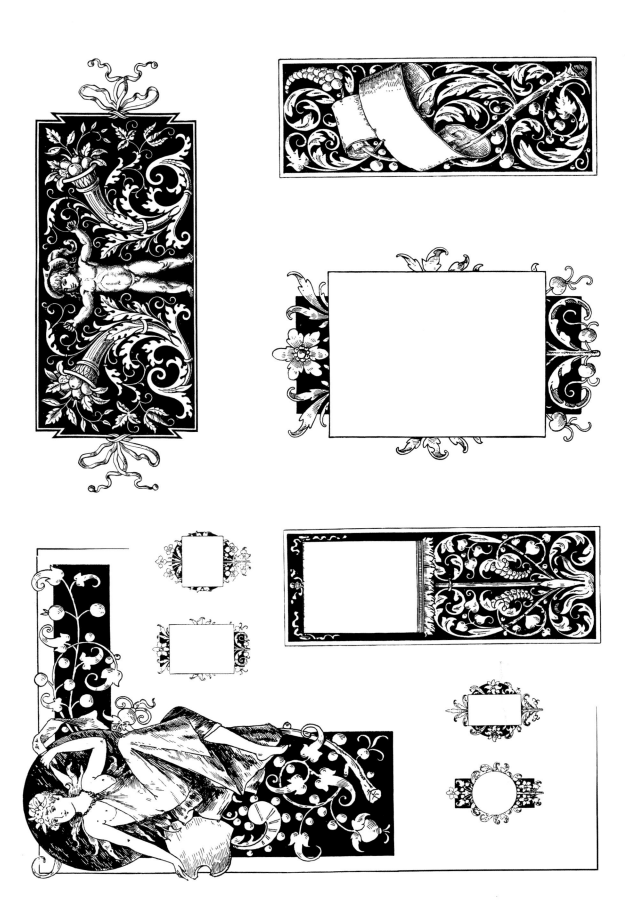

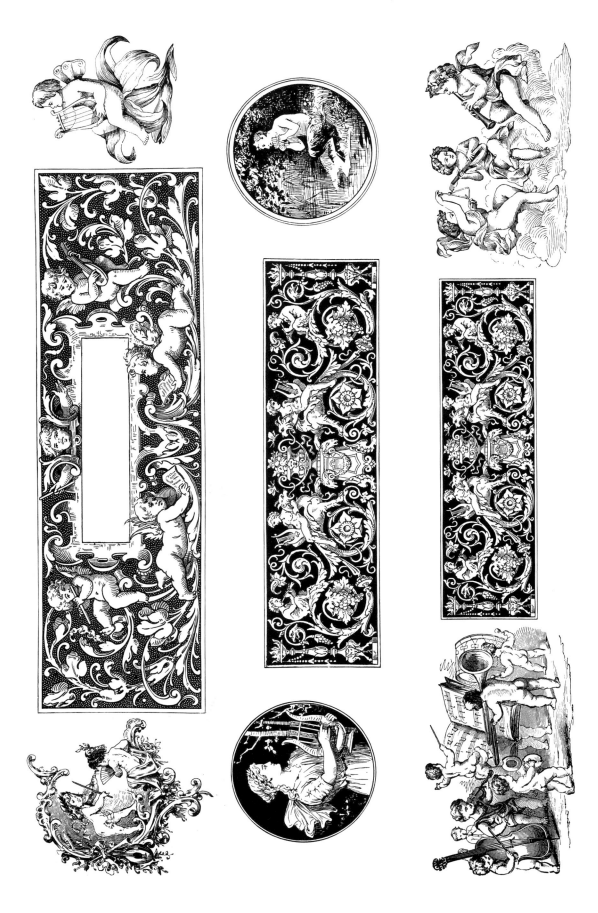

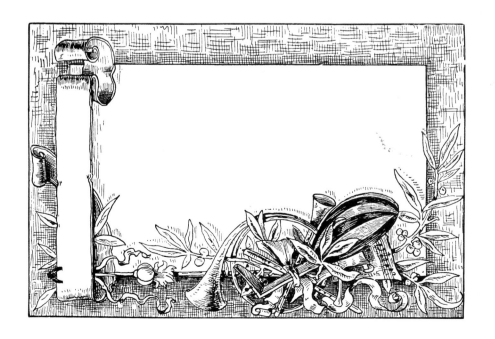

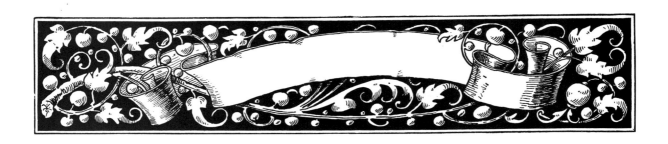

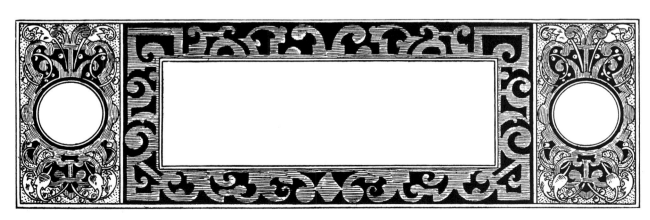

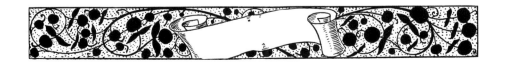

NÜRNBERGER SPIELWAREN-
FABRIK
BERNHARD HAUNSDORF
KAMENZ GEGRÜNDET
IM JAHR 1745

SPEDITIONS-GESCHÄFT
KONRAD DOMEYER
Prinz Albert-
Strasse 47 DRESDEN
Vertretung in allen Hauptstädten
des In- und Auslandes

NÄHMASCHINEN-FABRIK
Aktien-Gesellschaft
vorm. Bruno Eckhardt

Telegramm-Adresse:
Nähmaschinen-Wurzen
Fernsprecher No. 57 WURZEN, ... 19

HEINRICH SCHNEIDER

KUNSTANSTALT FÜR HOCHÄTZUNG UND
GALVANOPLASTISCHE VERVIELFÄLTIGUNG

J. G. SCHELTER & GIESECKE
LEIPZIG

MASCHINEN
UND APPARATE
FÜR ALLE ZWEIGE
DER LANDWIRT-
SCHAFT

Max Zirkel

vormals Börner & Meyer

MASCHINEN-FABRIK

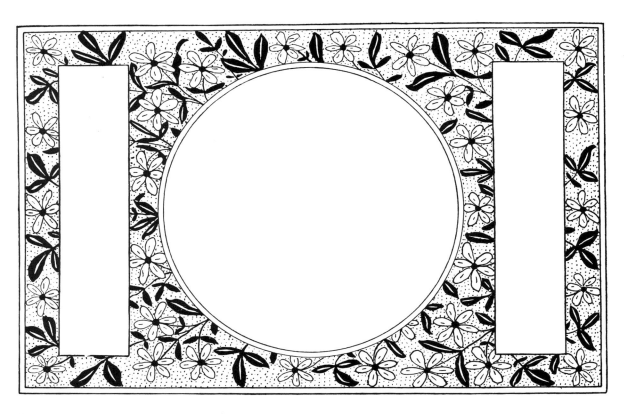

373

Herzlichen Glückwunsch zum Jahreswechsel

1901 Herzlichen Glückwunsch

Zum Jahreswechsel die besten Wünsche

Viel Glück im neuen Jahre.

Zum Jahreswechsel die besten Wünsche

Zum Jahreswechsel die besten Wünsche

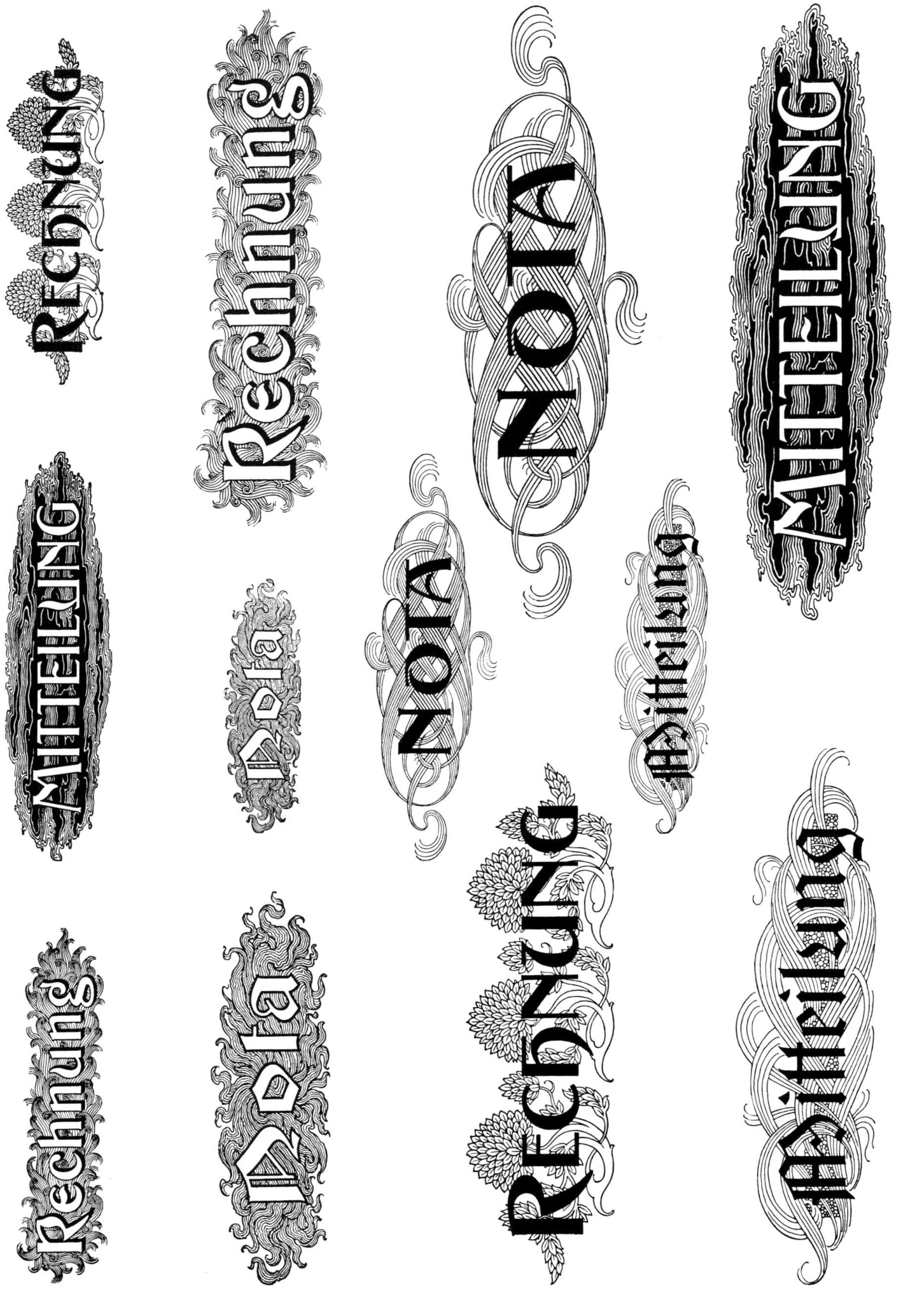

Rechnung

Rechnung

NOTA

MITTEILUNG

MITTEILUNG

Nota

NOTA

Mitteilung

Rechnung

Nota

Rechnung

Mitteilung

Factura

Mittheilung

Mittheilung

MEMORANDUM

Mittheilung

Memorandum

Mittheilung

Nota

Nota

Nota

Nota

Nota

Nota

Mittheilung

Mittheilung

MITTEILUNG

Memorandum

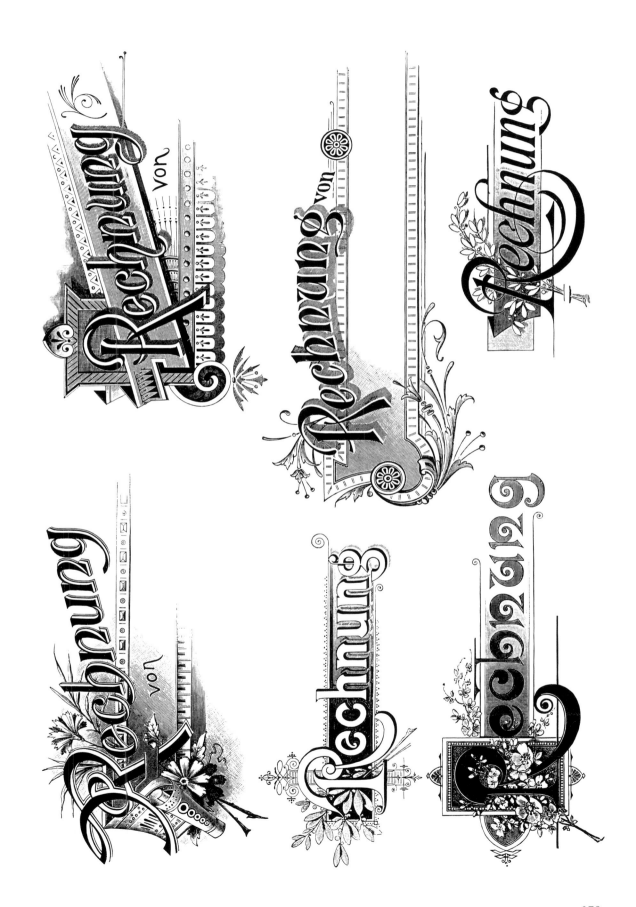

Mittheilung   Memorandum.   Mittheilung

Mittheilung Mittheilung Mittheilung Nota

Nota Nota Herr

Nota

Nota

Nota

Mittheilung

Nota von Nota

Nota

für Herr für Herr für Herr für Herr

Herr für Herr

für Herr

Rechnung

Faktura

Rechnung

Faktura

Rechnung

Rechnung

Faktur

Faktur

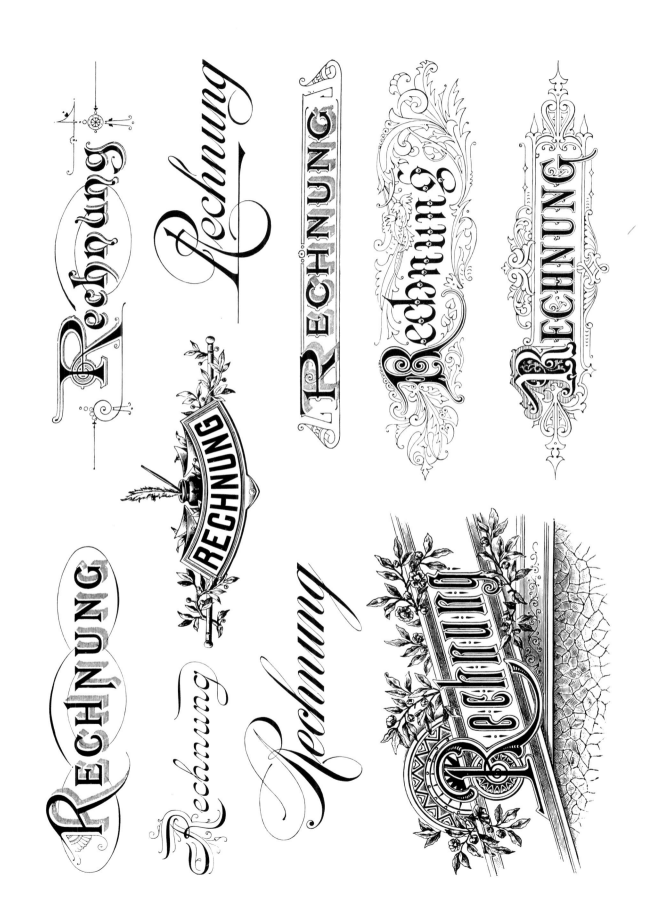

383

384

Herzlichen Glückwunsch zum Jahreswechsel

Herzlichen Glück zum neuen Jahr

Die herzlichsten Glückwünsche 1902

Viel Glück zum Neuen Jahre!

Herzlichsten

Glückwunsch

1902

Beste Gratulation

Herzliche Glückwünsche

1902

Herzliche Glückwünsche zum Jahreswechsel

Innigsten Glückwunsch zum Geburtstage!

1902

Die besten Wünsche zur Confirmation

Innigsten Glückwunsch

Die herzlichsten Wünsche zur Konfirmation

Innigsten Glückwunsch zum Jahreswechsel!

1902

Die besten Wünsche

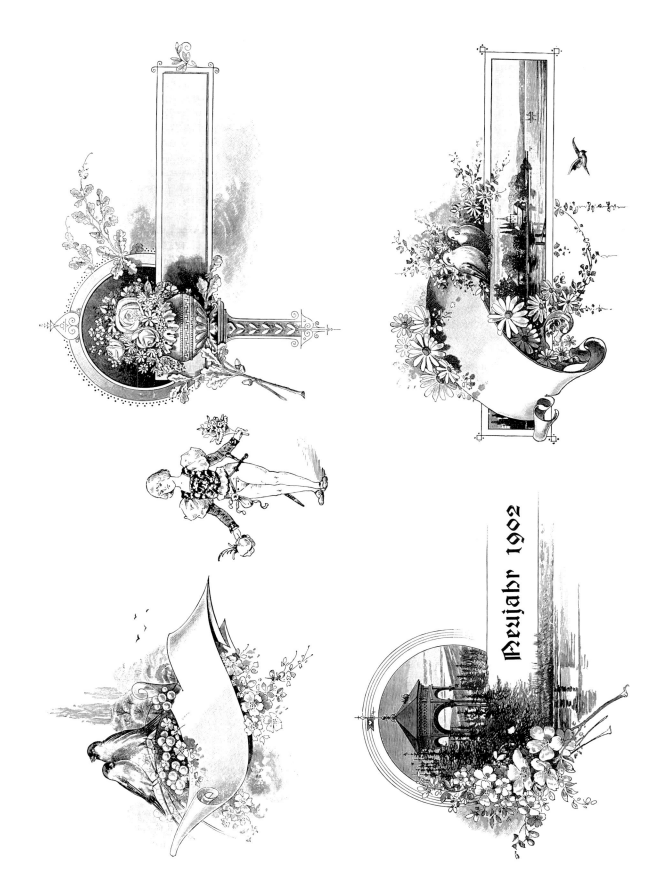

Neujahr 1902

Herzlichste GRATULATION

Herzliche Glückwünsche

DIE BESTEN Wünsche

Die besten Wünsche zum Jahreswechsel

Herzliche Gratulation zum Jahreswechsel!

DIE BESTEN WÜNSCHE Zum

Die besten Wünsche
zum
Jahreswechsel

Herzlichsten
Glückwunsch

Die herzlichsten Wünsche
zum
heutigen Tage

Herzlichen Glückwunsch
zum
neuen Jahre

Herzlichen
Glückwunsch

Herzliche Glückwünsche
zum Neuen Jahre